WILLIAM
SHAKESPEARE

MACBETH

CLASSICS

Published 2024

FiNGERPRINT! CLASSICS
Prakash Books

 Fingerprint Publishing
 @FingerprintP
 @fingerprintpublishingbooks
www.fingerprintpublishing.com

ISBN: 978 93 8917 851 7

William Shakespeare began his career as an actor, writer, and part owner of a playing company called the Lord Chamberlain's Men, later known as King's Men, in London. Often regarded as the 'Bard of Avon' he is one of the world's pre-eminent dramatists. Born and brought up in Stratford-upon-Avon, he married Anne Hathaway at the age of eighteen and they had three children—Susanna, and twins Hamnet and Judith. Though few records survive of his private life, he appeared to have retired to Stratford around 1613 where he died three years later.

His works still in existence, including some collaborations, consist of thirty-eight plays, one hundred and fifty-four sonnets, two long narrative poems, and several other verses. His plays are performed much more than any other playwright's and have been translated in almost all major languages. Most of his known works have been produced between 1589 and 1613. His early plays were mainly comedies and histories which remain regarded as some of the best works produced in these genres.

Shakespeare's plays are difficult to date. His early classical and Italianate comedies contain tight double plots and precise comic sequences giving way to the romantic atmosphere of his most acclaimed comedies in the mid-1590s. *A Midsummer Night's Dream*—a witty mixture of romance, fairy magic, and comic low life scenes—is one of his most delightful creations shortly before he turned to *Romeo and Juliet*. *Romeo and Juliet* is his most famous romantic tragedy of sexually charged adolescence, love, and death. It marks a departure from his earlier works and from others of the English Renaissance.

His plays demonstrate the expansiveness of his imagination and the extent of his learning. Shakespeare's sequence of great comedies continues with *Merchant of Venice*, *Much Ado About Nothing*, *As You Like It*, and *Twelfth Night*. He introduced prose comedy in the histories of the late 1590s—*Henry IV, Part I* and *Part II*, and *Henry V*—after the lyrical *Richard II*. *Julius Caesar* introduced a new kind of drama.

Shakespeare wrote the so-called 'problem plays' in the early 17th century. *Measure for Measure*, *Troilus and Cressida*, and *All's Well that Ends Well* being a few of them. Until about 1608, he mainly wrote tragedies including *Hamlet*, *Othello*, *King Lear*, and *Macbeth*. The story of a brave Scottish general named Macbeth, the eponymous drama illustrates how the lust for power dooms the fate of a noble person. When the trio of witches predict that Macbeth would eventually become the King of Scotland, his simmering ambitions overpower him, and persuaded by his wife he murders King Duncan and seizes the throne. But the play does not end here. In spite of being a man of guilt, he eventually becomes a tyrannical ruler. This Shakespearean tragedy has been adapted into multiple art forms across the centuries.

Antony and Cleopatra and *Coriolanus*—his last major tragedies, contain some of his finest poetry. Shakespeare wrote tragicomedies, also known as romances, in his last phase. These include *Cymbeline, The Winter's Tale,* and *The Tempest*, as well as the collaboration *Pericles, Prince of Tyre*.

A true genius, Shakespeare's popular characters and plots are studied, performed, reinterpreted, and discussed till today. William Shakespeare, known as the English national poet, is considered the greatest dramatist of all time.

CHARACTERS OF THE PLAY

DUNCAN, King of Scotland

MACBETH, Thane of Glamis and Cawdor, a general in the King's army

LADY MACBETH, his wife

MACDUFF, Thane of Fife, a nobleman of Scotland.

LADY MACDUFF, his wife

MALCOLM, elder son of Duncan

DONALBAIN, younger son of Duncan

BANQUO, Thane of Lochaber, a general in the King's army

FLEANCE, his son

LENNOX, ROSS, MENTEITH, ANGUS, CAITHNESS, noblemen of Scotland

SIWARD, Earl of Northumberland, general of the English forces

YOUNG SIWARD, his son

SEYTON, attendant to Macbeth

HECATE, Queen of the Witches
Witches
BOY, Son of Macduff
Gentlewoman attending on Lady Macbeth
An English Doctor
A Scottish Doctor
A Sergeant
A Porter
An Old Man
The Ghost of Banquo and other Apparitions
Lords, Gentlemen, Officers, Soldiers, Murtherers,
Attendants, and Messengers

SCENE:
SCOTLAND AND ENGLAND

Act I

SCENE I. A DESERT PLACE.

Thunder and lightning. Enter three Witches

FIRST WITCH

    When shall we three meet again

    In thunder, lightning, or in rain?

SECOND WITCH

    When the hurlyburly's done,

    When the battle's lost and won.

THIRD WITCH

    That will be ere the set of sun.

FIRST WITCH

    Where the place?

SECOND WITCH

    Upon the heath.

THIRD WITCH

    There to meet with Macbeth.

FIRST WITCH

I come, Graymalkin!

SECOND WITCH

Paddock calls.

THIRD WITCH

Anon.

ALL

Fair is foul, and foul is fair:

Hover through the fog and filthy air.

Exeunt

SCENE II. A CAMP NEAR FORRES.

Alarum within.

Enter Duncan, Malcolm, Donalbain, Lennox, with Attendants, meeting a bleeding Sergeant

DUNCAN

What bloody man is that? He can report,

As seemeth by his plight, of the revolt

The newest state.

MALCOLM

This is the sergeant

Who like a good and hardy soldier fought

'Gainst my captivity. Hail, brave friend!

Say to the king the knowledge of the broil

As thou didst leave it.

SERGEANT

    Doubtful it stood;

    As two spent swimmers, that do cling together

    And choke their art. The merciless
        Macdonwald—

    Worthy to be a rebel, for to that

    The multiplying villanies of nature

    Do swarm upon him—from the western isles

    Of kerns and gallowglasses is supplied;

    And fortune, on his damned quarrel smiling,

    Show'd like a rebel's whore: but all's too weak:

    For brave Macbeth—well he deserves that
        name—

    Disdaining fortune, with his brandish'd steel,

    Which smoked with bloody execution,

    Like valour's minion carved out his passage

    Till he faced the slave;

    Which ne'er shook hands, nor bade farewell to
        him,

    Till he unseam'd him from the nave to the
        chaps,

    And fix'd his head upon our battlements.

DUNCAN

    O valiant cousin! worthy gentleman!

SERGEANT

    As whence the sun 'gins his reflection

Shipwrecking storms and direful thunders
    break,
So from that spring whence comfort seem'd to
    come
Discomfort swells. Mark, king of Scotland,
    mark:
No sooner justice had with valour arm'd
Compell'd these skipping kerns to trust their
    heels,
But the Norweyan lord surveying vantage,
With furbish'd arms and new supplies of men
Began a fresh assault.

DUNCAN

    Dismay'd not this
    Our captains, Macbeth and Banquo?

SERGEANT

    Yes;
    As sparrows eagles, or the hare the lion.
    If I say sooth, I must report they were
    As cannons overcharged with double cracks,
        so they
    Doubly redoubled strokes upon the foe:
    Except they meant to bathe in reeking wounds,
    Or memorise another Golgotha,
    I cannot tell.
    But I am faint, my gashes cry for help.

DUNCAN

So well thy words become thee as thy wounds;

They smack of honour both. Go get him
surgeons.

Exit Sergeant, attended

Who comes here?

Enter Ross

MALCOLM

The worthy thane of Ross.

LENNOX

What a haste looks through his eyes! So should
he look

That seems to speak things strange.

ROSS

God save the king!

DUNCAN

Whence camest thou, worthy thane?

ROSS

From Fife, great king;

Where the Norweyan banners flout the sky

And fan our people cold. Norway himself,

With terrible numbers,

Assisted by that most disloyal traitor

The thane of Cawdor, began a dismal conflict;

Till that Bellona's bridegroom, lapp'd in proof,

Confronted him with self-comparisons,

Point against point rebellious, arm 'gainst arm.
Curbing his lavish spirit: and, to conclude,
The victory fell on us.

DUNCAN

Great happiness!

ROSS

That now
Sweno, the Norways' king, craves composition:
Nor would we deign him burial of his men
Till he disbursed at Saint Colme's inch
Ten thousand dollars to our general use.

DUNCAN

No more that thane of Cawdor shall deceive
Our bosom interest: go pronounce his present
  death,
And with his former title greet Macbeth.

ROSS

I'll see it done.

DUNCAN

What he hath lost noble Macbeth hath won.

Exeunt

SCENE III. A HEATH NEAR FORRES.

Thunder. Enter the three Witches

FIRST WITCH

Where hast thou been, sister?

SECOND WITCH

Killing swine.

THIRD WITCH

Sister, where thou?

FIRST WITCH

A sailor's wife had chestnuts in her lap,

And munch'd, and munch'd, and munch'd:—

'Give me,' quoth I:

'Aroint thee, witch!' the rump-fed ronyon cries.

Her husband's to Aleppo gone, master o'the

Tiger:

But in a sieve I'll thither sail,

And, like a rat without a tail,

I'll do, I'll do, and I'll do.

SECOND WITCH

I'll give thee a wind.

FIRST WITCH

Thou'rt kind.

THIRD WITCH

And I another.

FIRST WITCH

I myself have all the other,

And the very ports they blow,

All the quarters that they know

I'the shipman's card.

I will drain him dry as hay:

Sleep shall neither night nor day

Hang upon his pent-house lid;
He shall live a man forbid:
Weary se'nnights nine times nine
Shall he dwindle, peak and pine:
Though his bark cannot be lost,
Yet it shall be tempest-tost.
Look what I have.

SECOND WITCH

Show me, show me.

FIRST WITCH

Here I have a pilot's thumb,
Wreck'd as homeward he did come.

Drum within

THIRD WITCH

A drum, a drum!
Macbeth doth come.

ALL

The weird sisters, hand in hand,
Posters of the sea and land,
Thus do go about, about:
Thrice to thine and thrice to mine
And thrice again, to make up nine.
Peace! the charm's wound up.

Enter Macbeth and Banquo

MACBETH

So foul and fair a day I have not seen.

BANQUO

How far is't call'd to Forres? What are these
So wither'd and so wild in their attire,
That look not like the inhabitants o'the earth,
And yet are on't? Live you? or are you aught
That man may question? You seem to
understand me,
By each at once her chappy finger laying
Upon her skinny lips: you should be women,
And yet your beards forbid me to interpret
That you are so.

MACBETH

Speak, if you can: what are you?

FIRST WITCH

All hail, Macbeth! hail to thee, thane of Glamis!

SECOND WITCH

All hail, Macbeth, hail to thee, thane of
Cawdor!

THIRD WITCH

All hail, Macbeth, thou shalt be king hereafter!

BANQUO

Good sir, why do you start; and seem to fear
Things that do sound so fair? I'the name of
truth,
Are ye fantastical, or that indeed
Which outwardly ye show? My noble partner

You greet with present grace and great prediction
Of noble having and of royal hope,
That he seems rapt withal: to me you speak not.
If you can look into the seeds of time,
And say which grain will grow and which will not,
Speak then to me, who neither beg nor fear
Your favours nor your hate.

FIRST WITCH

Hail!

SECOND WITCH

Hail!

THIRD WITCH

Hail!

FIRST WITCH

Lesser than Macbeth, and greater.

SECOND WITCH

Not so happy, yet much happier.

THIRD WITCH

Thou shalt get kings, though thou be none:
So all hail, Macbeth and Banquo!

FIRST WITCH

Banquo and Macbeth, all hail!

MACBETH

Stay, you imperfect speakers, tell me more:
By Sinel's death I know I am thane of Glamis;

But how of Cawdor? the thane of Cawdor lives,
A prosperous gentleman; and to be king
Stands not within the prospect of belief,
No more than to be Cawdor. Say from whence
You owe this strange intelligence? or why
Upon this blasted heath you stop our way
With such prophetic greeting? Speak, I charge
  you.

   Witches vanish

BANQUO

The earth hath bubbles, as the water has,
And these are of them. Whither are they
  vanish'd?

MACBETH

Into the air; and what seem'd corporal melted
As breath into the wind. Would they had stay'd!

BANQUO

Were such things here as we do speak about?
Or have we eaten on the insane root
That takes the reason prisoner?

MACBETH

Your children shall be kings.

BANQUO

You shall be king.

MACBETH

And thane of Cawdor too: went it not so?

BANQUO

> To the selfsame tune and words. Who's here?
>
> *Enter Ross and Angus*

ROSS

> The king hath happily received, Macbeth,
> The news of thy success; and when he reads
> Thy personal venture in the rebels' fight,
> His wonders and his praises do contend
> Which should be thine or his: silenced with
>   that,
> In viewing o'er the rest o'the selfsame day,
> He finds thee in the stout Norweyan ranks,
> Nothing afeard of what thyself didst make,
> Strange images of death. As thick as hail
> Came post with post; and every one did bear
> Thy praises in his kingdom's great defence,
> And pour'd them down before him.

ANGUS

> We are sent
> To give thee from our royal master thanks;
> Only to herald thee into his sight,
> Not pay thee.

ROSS

> And, for an earnest of a greater honour,
> He bade me, from him, call thee thane of Cawdor:
> In which addition, hail, most worthy thane!
> For it is thine.

BANQUO

What, can the devil speak true?

MACBETH

The thane of Cawdor lives: why do you dress me

In borrow'd robes?

ANGUS

Who was the thane lives yet;

But under heavy judgment bears that life

Which he deserves to lose. Whether he was

combined

With those of Norway, or did line the rebel

With hidden help and vantage, or that with

both

He labour'd in his country's wreck, I know not;

But treasons capital, confess'd and proved,

Have overthrown him.

MACBETH

[*Aside*] Glamis, and thane of Cawdor!

The greatest is behind.

To Ross and Angus

Thanks for your pains.

To Banquo

Do you not hope your children shall be kings,

When those that gave the thane of Cawdor to me

Promised no less to them?

BANQUO

That trusted home

Might yet enkindle you unto the crown,
Besides the thane of Cawdor. But 'tis strange:
And oftentimes, to win us to our harm,
The instruments of darkness tell us truths,
Win us with honest trifles, to betray's
In deepest consequence.
Cousins, a word, I pray you.

MACBETH

[*Aside*] Two truths are told,
As happy prologues to the swelling act
Of the imperial theme.—I thank you, gentlemen.

    [*Aside*] This supernatural soliciting
Cannot be ill, cannot be good: if ill,
Why hath it given me earnest of success,
Commencing in a truth? I am thane of Cawdor:
If good, why do I yield to that suggestion
Whose horrid image doth unfix my hair
And make my seated heart knock at my ribs,
Against the use of nature? Present fears
Are less than horrible imaginings:
My thought, whose murder yet is but fantastical,
Shakes so my single state of man that function
Is smother'd in surmise, and nothing is
But what is not.

BANQUO

Look, how our partner's rapt.

MACBETH

[*Aside*] If chance will have me king, why, chance
may crown me,
Without my stir.

BANQUO

New horrors come upon him,
Like our strange garments, cleave not to their
mould
But with the aid of use.

MACBETH

[*Aside*] Come what come may,
Time and the hour runs through the roughest
day.

BANQUO

Worthy Macbeth, we stay upon your leisure.

MACBETH

Give me your favour: my dull brain was wrought
With things forgotten. Kind gentlemen, your
pains
Are register'd where every day I turn
The leaf to read them. Let us toward the king.
Think upon what hath chanced, and, at more
time,
The interim having weigh'd it, let us speak
Our free hearts each to other.

BANQUO

Very gladly.

MACBETH

Till then, enough. Come, friends.

Exeunt

SCENE IV. FORRES. THE PALACE.

Flourish. Enter Duncan, Malcolm, Donalbain, Lennox, and Attendants

DUNCAN

Is execution done on Cawdor? Are not
Those in commission yet return'd?

MALCOLM

My liege,
They are not yet come back. But I have spoke
With one that saw him die: who did report
That very frankly he confess'd his treasons,
Implored your highness' pardon and set forth
A deep repentance: nothing in his life
Became him like the leaving it; he died
As one that had been studied in his death
To throw away the dearest thing he owed,
As 'twere a careless trifle.

DUNCAN

There's no art
To find the mind's construction in the face:
He was a gentleman on whom I built
An absolute trust.

Enter Macbeth, Banquo, Ross, and Angus

O worthiest cousin!

The sin of my ingratitude even now

Was heavy on me: thou art so far before

That swiftest wing of recompense is slow

To overtake thee. Would thou hadst less
deserved,

That the proportion both of thanks and
payment

Might have been mine! only I have left to say,

More is thy due than more than all can pay.

MACBETH

The service and the loyalty I owe,

In doing it, pays itself. Your highness' part

Is to receive our duties; and our duties

Are to your throne and state children and
servants,

Which do but what they should, by doing every
thing

Safe toward your love and honour.

DUNCAN

Welcome hither:

I have begun to plant thee, and will labour

To make thee full of growing. Noble Banquo,

That hast no less deserved, nor must be known

No less to have done so, let me enfold thee

And hold thee to my heart.

BANQUO

There if I grow,
The harvest is your own.

DUNCAN

My plenteous joys,
Wanton in fulness, seek to hide themselves
In drops of sorrow. Sons, kinsmen, thanes,
And you whose places are the nearest, know
We will establish our estate upon
Our eldest, Malcolm, whom we name hereafter
The Prince of Cumberland; which honour must
Not unaccompanied invest him only,
But signs of nobleness, like stars, shall shine
On all deservers. From hence to Inverness,
And bind us further to you.

MACBETH

The rest is labour, which is not used for you:
I'll be myself the harbinger and make joyful
The hearing of my wife with your approach;
So humbly take my leave.

DUNCAN

My worthy Cawdor!

MACBETH

[*Aside*] The Prince of Cumberland! that is a step
On which I must fall down, or else o'erleap,
For in my way it lies. Stars, hide your fires;

Let not light see my black and deep desires:
The eye wink at the hand; yet let that be,
Which the eye fears, when it is done, to see.

Exit

DUNCAN

True, worthy Banquo; he is full so valiant,
And in his commendations I am fed;
It is a banquet to me. Let's after him,
Whose care is gone before to bid us welcome:
It is a peerless kinsman.

Flourish. Exeunt

SCENE V. INVERNESS.
MACBETH'S CASTLE.

Enter Lady Macbeth, reading a letter
LADY MACBETH

'*They met me in the day of success: and I have learned
by the perfectest report, they have more in them than
mortal knowledge. When I burned in desire to question
them further, they made themselves air, into which they
vanished. Whiles I stood rapt in the wonder of it, came
missives from the king, who all-hailed me "Thane of
Cawdor;" by which title, before, these weird sisters
saluted me, and referred me to the coming on of time,
with "Hail, king that shalt be!" This have I thought
good to deliver thee, my dearest partner of greatness,*

that thou mightst not lose the dues of rejoicing, by being
ignorant of what greatness is promised thee. Lay it to
thy heart, and farewell.'

Glamis thou art, and Cawdor; and shalt be
What thou art promised: yet do I fear thy nature;
It is too full o'the milk of human kindness
To catch the nearest way: thou wouldst be great;
Art not without ambition, but without
The illness should attend it: what thou wouldst
  highly,
That wouldst thou holily; wouldst not play false,
And yet wouldst wrongly win: thou'ldst have,
  great Glamis,
That which cries 'Thus thou must do, if thou
  have it;
And that which rather thou dost fear to do
Than wishest should be undone.' Hie thee
  hither,
That I may pour my spirits in thine ear;
And chastise with the valour of my tongue
All that impedes thee from the golden round,
Which fate and metaphysical aid doth seem
To have thee crown'd withal.
    Enter a Messenger
What is your tidings?
MESSENGER
The king comes here to-night.

LADY MACBETH

    Thou'rt mad to say it:

    Is not thy master with him? who, were't so,

    Would have inform'd for preparation.

MESSENGER

    So please you, it is true: our thane is coming:

    One of my fellows had the speed of him,

    Who, almost dead for breath, had scarcely more

    Than would make up his message.

LADY MACBETH

    Give him tending;

    He brings great news.

Exit Messenger

    The raven himself is hoarse

    That croaks the fatal entrance of Duncan

    Under my battlements. Come, you spirits

    That tend on mortal thoughts, unsex me here,

    And fill me from the crown to the toe top-full

    Of direst cruelty! make thick my blood;

    Stop up the access and passage to remorse,

    That no compunctious visitings of nature

    Shake my fell purpose, nor keep peace between

    The effect and it! Come to my woman's breasts,

    And take my milk for gall, you murdering ministers,

    Wherever in your sightless substances

    You wait on nature's mischief! Come, thick night,

31

And pall thee in the dunnest smoke of hell,
That my keen knife see not the wound it makes,
Nor heaven peep through the blanket of the
    dark,
To cry 'Hold, hold!'
            Enter Macbeth
Great Glamis! worthy Cawdor!
Greater than both, by the all-hail hereafter!
Thy letters have transported me beyond
This ignorant present, and I feel now
The future in the instant.
MACBETH
    My dearest love,
    Duncan comes here to-night.
LADY MACBETH
    And when goes hence?
MACBETH
    To-morrow, as he purposes.
LADY MACBETH
    O, never
Shall sun that morrow see!
Your face, my thane, is as a book where men
May read strange matters. To beguile the time,
Look like the time; bear welcome in your eye,
Your hand, your tongue: look like the innocent
    flower,
But be the serpent under't. He that's coming

Must be provided for: and you shall put
This night's great business into my dispatch;
Which shall to all our nights and days to come
Give solely sovereign sway and masterdom.

MACBETH

We will speak further.

LADY MACBETH

Only look up clear;
To alter favour ever is to fear:
Leave all the rest to me.

Exeunt

SCENE VI. BEFORE MACBETH'S CASTLE.

*Hautboys and torches. Enter Duncan, Malcolm, Donalbain,
Banquo, Lennox, Macduff, Ross, Angus, and Attendants*

DUNCAN

This castle hath a pleasant seat; the air
Nimbly and sweetly recommends itself
Unto our gentle senses.

BANQUO

This guest of summer,
The temple-haunting martlet, does approve,
By his loved mansionry, that the heaven's breath
Smells wooingly here: no jutty, frieze,
Buttress, nor coign of vantage, but this bird
Hath made his pendent bed and procreant cradle:

Where they most breed and haunt, I have observed,
The air is delicate.

Enter Lady Macbeth

DUNCAN

See, see, our honour'd hostess!
The love that follows us sometime is our trouble,
Which still we thank as love. Herein I teach you
How you shall bid God 'ild us for your pains,
And thank us for your trouble.

LADY MACBETH

All our service
In every point twice done and then done double
Were poor and single business to contend
Against those honours deep and broad wherewith
Your majesty loads our house: for those of old,
And the late dignities heap'd up to them,
We rest your hermits.

DUNCAN

Where's the thane of Cawdor?
We coursed him at the heels, and had a purpose
To be his purveyor: but he rides well;
And his great love, sharp as his spur, hath holp him
To his home before us. Fair and noble hostess,
We are your guest to-night.

LADY MACBETH

    Your servants ever

    Have theirs, themselves and what is theirs, in
        compt,

    To make their audit at your highness' pleasure,

    Still to return your own.

DUNCAN

    Give me your hand;

    Conduct me to mine host: we love him highly,

    And shall continue our graces towards him.

    By your leave, hostess.

Exeunt

SCENE VII. MACBETH'S CASTLE.

Hautboys and torches. Enter a Sewer, and divers Servants with dishes and service, and pass over the stage. Then enter Macbeth

MACBETH

    If it were done when 'tis done, then 'twere well

    It were done quickly: if the assassination

    Could trammel up the consequence, and catch

    With his surcease success; that but this blow

    Might be the be-all and the end-all here,

    But here, upon this bank and shoal of time,

    We'ld jump the life to come. But in these cases

    We still have judgment here; that we but teach

Bloody instructions, which, being taught, return
To plague the inventor: this even-handed justice
Commends the ingredients of our poison'd chalice
To our own lips. He's here in double trust;
First, as I am his kinsman and his subject,
Strong both against the deed; then, as his host,
Who should against his murderer shut the door,
Not bear the knife myself. Besides, this Duncan
Hath borne his faculties so meek, hath been
So clear in his great office, that his virtues
Will plead like angels, trumpet-tongued, against
The deep damnation of his taking-off;
And pity, like a naked new-born babe,
Striding the blast, or heaven's cherubim, horsed
Upon the sightless couriers of the air,
Shall blow the horrid deed in every eye,
That tears shall drown the wind. I have no spur
To prick the sides of my intent, but only
Vaulting ambition, which o'erleaps itself
And falls on the other.

Enter Lady Macbeth

How now! what news?

LADY MACBETH

He has almost supp'd: why have you left the chamber?

MACBETH

    Hath he ask'd for me?

LADY MACBETH

    Know you not he has?

MACBETH

    We will proceed no further in this business:

    He hath honour'd me of late; and I have bought

    Golden opinions from all sorts of people,

    Which would be worn now in their newest
        gloss,

    Not cast aside so soon.

LADY MACBETH

    Was the hope drunk

    Wherein you dress'd yourself? hath it slept since?

    And wakes it now, to look so green and pale

    At what it did so freely? From this time

    Such I account thy love. Art thou afeard

    To be the same in thine own act and valour

    As thou art in desire? Wouldst thou have that

    Which thou esteem'st the ornament of life,

    And live a coward in thine own esteem,

    Letting 'I dare not' wait upon 'I would,'

    Like the poor cat i'the adage?

MACBETH

    Prithee, peace:

    I dare do all that may become a man;

    Who dares do more is none.

LADY MACBETH
>What beast was't, then,
>That made you break this enterprise to me?
>When you durst do it, then you were a man;
>And, to be more than what you were, you would
>Be so much more the man. Nor time nor place
>Did then adhere, and yet you would make both:
>They have made themselves, and that their
>>fitness now
>Does unmake you. I have given suck, and know
>How tender 'tis to love the babe that milks me:
>I would, while it was smiling in my face,
>Have pluck'd my nipple from his boneless gums,
>And dash'd the brains out, had I so sworn as
>>you
>Have done to this.

MACBETH
>If we should fail?

LADY MACBETH
>We fail!
>But screw your courage to the sticking-place,
>And we'll not fail. When Duncan is asleep—
>Whereto the rather shall his day's hard journey
>Soundly invite him—his two chamberlains
>Will I with wine and wassail so convince
>That memory, the warder of the brain,
>Shall be a fume, and the receipt of reason

A limbeck only: when in swinish sleep
Their drenched natures lie as in a death,
What cannot you and I perform upon
The unguarded Duncan? what not put upon
His spongy officers, who shall bear the guilt
Of our great quell?

MACBETH

Bring forth men-children only;
For thy undaunted mettle should compose
Nothing but males. Will it not be received,
When we have mark'd with blood those sleepy
    two
Of his own chamber and used their very daggers,
That they have done't?

LADY MACBETH

Who dares receive it other,
As we shall make our griefs and clamour roar
Upon his death?

MACBETH

I am settled, and bend up
Each corporal agent to this terrible feat.
Away, and mock the time with fairest show:
False face must hide what the false heart doth
    know.

Exeunt

***

Act II

SCENE I. COURT OF MACBETH'S CASTLE.

Enter Banquo, and Fleance bearing a torch before him

BANQUO

How goes the night, boy?

FLEANCE

The moon is down; I have not heard the clock.

BANQUO

And she goes down at twelve.

FLEANCE

I take't, 'tis later, sir.

BANQUO

Hold, take my sword. There's husbandry in heaven;
Their candles are all out. Take thee that too.
A heavy summons lies like lead upon me,
And yet I would not sleep: merciful powers,
Restrain in me the cursed thoughts that nature

Gives way to in repose!

Enter Macbeth, and a Servant with a torch

Give me my sword.

Who's there?

MACBETH

A friend.

BANQUO

What, sir, not yet at rest? The king's a-bed:

He hath been in unusual pleasure, and

Sent forth great largess to your offices.

This diamond he greets your wife withal,

By the name of most kind hostess; and shut up

In measureless content.

MACBETH

Being unprepared,

Our will became the servant to defect;

Which else should free have wrought.

BANQUO

All's well.

I dreamt last night of the three weird sisters:

To you they have show'd some truth.

MACBETH

I think not of them:

Yet, when we can entreat an hour to serve,

We would spend it in some words upon that
	business,

If you would grant the time.

BANQUO

At your kind'st leisure.

MACBETH

If you shall cleave to my consent, when 'tis,

It shall make honour for you.

BANQUO

So I lose none

In seeking to augment it, but still keep

My bosom franchised and allegiance clear,

I shall be counsell'd.

MACBETH

Good repose the while!

BANQUO

Thanks, sir: the like to you!

Exeunt Banquo and Fleance

MACBETH

Go bid thy mistress, when my drink is ready,

She strike upon the bell. Get thee to bed.

Exit Servant

Is this a dagger which I see before me,

The handle toward my hand? Come, let me clutch thee.

I have thee not, and yet I see thee still.

Art thou not, fatal vision, sensible

To feeling as to sight? or art thou but

A dagger of the mind, a false creation,

Proceeding from the heat-oppressed brain?

I see thee yet, in form as palpable
As this which now I draw.
Thou marshall'st me the way that I was going;
And such an instrument I was to use.
Mine eyes are made the fools o'the other senses,
Or else worth all the rest; I see thee still,
And on thy blade and dudgeon gouts of blood,
Which was not so before. There's no such thing:
It is the bloody business which informs
Thus to mine eyes. Now o'er the one halfworld
Nature seems dead, and wicked dreams abuse
The curtain'd sleep; witchcraft celebrates
Pale Hecate's offerings, and wither'd murder,
Alarum'd by his sentinel, the wolf,
Whose howl's his watch, thus with his stealthy
    pace.
With Tarquin's ravishing strides, towards his
    design
Moves like a ghost. Thou sure and firm-set
    earth,
Hear not my steps, which way they walk, for fear
Thy very stones prate of my whereabout,
And take the present horror from the time,
Which now suits with it. Whiles I threat, he
    lives:
Words to the heat of deeds too cold breath
    gives.

A bell rings

I go, and it is done; the bell invites me.

Hear it not, Duncan; for it is a knell

That summons thee to heaven or to hell.

Exit

SCENE II. THE SAME.

Enter Lady Macbeth

LADY MACBETH

That which hath made them drunk hath made
me bold;

What hath quench'd them hath given me fire.
Hark! Peace!

It was the owl that shriek'd, the fatal bellman,

Which gives the stern'st good-night. He is
about it:

The doors are open; and the surfeited grooms

Do mock their charge with snores: I have
drugg'd their possets,

That death and nature do contend about them,

Whether they live or die.

MACBETH

[*Within*] Who's there? what, ho!

LADY MACBETH

Alack, I am afraid they have awaked,

And 'tis not done. The attempt and not the
    deed
Confounds us. Hark! I laid their daggers ready;
He could not miss 'em. Had he not resembled
My father as he slept, I had done't.

Enter Macbeth

My husband!

MACBETH

I have done the deed. Didst thou not hear a
noise?

LADY MACBETH

I heard the owl scream and the crickets cry.
Did not you speak?

MACBETH

When?

LADY MACBETH

Now.

MACBETH

As I descended?

LADY MACBETH

Ay.

MACBETH

Hark!
Who lies i'the second chamber?

LADY MACBETH

Donalbain.

MACBETH

This is a sorry sight.

Looking on his hands

LADY MACBETH

A foolish thought, to say a sorry sight.

MACBETH

There's one did laugh in's sleep, and one cried
'Murder!'

That they did wake each other: I stood and
heard them:

But they did say their prayers, and address'd
them

Again to sleep.

LADY MACBETH

There are two lodged together.

MACBETH

One cried 'God bless us!' and 'Amen' the other;

As they had seen me with these hangman's hands.

Listening their fear, I could not say 'Amen,'

When they did say 'God bless us!'

LADY MACBETH

Consider it not so deeply.

MACBETH

But wherefore could not I pronounce 'Amen'?

I had most need of blessing, and 'Amen'

Stuck in my throat.

LADY MACBETH

These deeds must not be thought

After these ways; so, it will make us mad.

MACBETH

Methought I heard a voice cry 'sleep no more!

Macbeth does murder sleep', the innocent
sleep,

Sleep that knits up the ravell'd sleeve of care,

The death of each day's life, sore labour's bath,

Balm of hurt minds, great nature's second
course,

Chief nourisher in life's feast'

LADY MACBETH

What do you mean?

MACBETH

Still it cried 'sleep no more!' to all the house:

'Glamis hath murder'd sleep, and therefore
Cawdor

Shall sleep no more; Macbeth shall sleep no
more.'

LADY MACBETH

Who was it that thus cried? Why, worthy thane,

You do unbend your noble strength, to think

So brainsickly of things. Go get some water,

And wash this filthy witness from your hand.

Why did you bring these daggers from the
place?

They must lie there: go carry them; and smear
The sleepy grooms with blood.

MACBETH

I'll go no more:
I am afraid to think what I have done;
Look on't again I dare not.

LADY MACBETH

Infirm of purpose!
Give me the daggers: the sleeping and the dead
Are but as pictures: 'tis the eye of childhood
That fears a painted devil. If he do bleed,
I'll gild the faces of the grooms withal;
For it must seem their guilt.

Exit. Knocking within

MACBETH

Whence is that knocking?
How is't with me, when every noise appals me?
What hands are here? ha! they pluck out mine
eyes.
Will all great Neptune's ocean wash this blood
Clean from my hand? No, this my hand will
rather
The multitudinous seas in incarnadine,
Making the green one red.

Re-enter Lady Macbeth

LADY MACBETH

My hands are of your colour; but I shame

To wear a heart so white.

Knocking within

I hear a knocking
At the south entry: retire we to our chamber;
A little water clears us of this deed:
How easy is it, then! Your constancy
Hath left you unattended.

Knocking within

Hark! more knocking.
Get on your nightgown, lest occasion call us,
And show us to be watchers. Be not lost
So poorly in your thoughts.

MACBETH

To know my deed, 'twere best not know myself.

Knocking within

Wake Duncan with thy knocking! I would thou
couldst!

Exeunt

SCENE III. THE SAME.

Knocking within. Enter a Porter

PORTER

Here's a knocking indeed! If a man were
porter of hell-gate, he should have old turning
the key.

Knocking within

Knock, knock, knock! Who's there, i'the name of Beelzebub? Here's a farmer, that hanged himself on the expectation of plenty: come in time; have napkins enow about you; here you'll sweat for't.

Knocking within

Knock, knock! Who's there, in the other devil's name? Faith, here's an equivocator, that could swear in both the scales against either scale; who committed treason enough for God's sake, yet could not equivocate to heaven: O, come in, equivocator.

Knocking within

Knock, knock, knock! Who's there? Faith, here's an English tailor come hither, for stealing out of a French hose: come in, tailor; here you may roast your goose.

Knocking within

Knock, knock; never at quiet! What are you? But this place is too cold for hell. I'll devil-porter it no further: I had thought to have let in some of all professions that go the primrose way to the everlasting bonfire.

Knocking within

Anon, anon! I pray you, remember the porter.

Opens the gate.
Enter Macduff and Lennox

MACDUFF

Was it so late, friend, ere you went to bed,

That you do lie so late?

PORTER

'Faith sir, we were carousing till the second
cock: and drink, sir, is a great provoker of three
things.

MACDUFF

What three things does drink especially
provoke?

PORTER

Marry, sir, nose-painting, sleep, and urine.
Lechery, sir, it provokes, and unprovokes;
it provokes the desire, but it takes away the
performance: therefore, much drink may
be said to be an equivocator with lechery: it
makes him, and it mars him; it sets him on,
and it takes him off; it persuades him, and
disheartens him; makes him stand to, and not
stand to; in conclusion, equivocates him in a
sleep, and, giving him the lie, leaves him.

MACDUFF

I believe drink gave thee the lie last night.

PORTER

That it did, sir, i'the very throat on me: but
I requited him for his lie; and, I think, being

too strong for him, though he took up my legs
sometime, yet I made a shift to cast him.

MACDUFF

Is thy master stirring?

Enter Macbeth

Our knocking has awaked him; here he comes.

LENNOX

Good morrow, noble sir.

MACBETH

Good morrow, both.

MACDUFF

Is the king stirring, worthy thane?

MACBETH

Not yet.

MACDUFF

He did command me to call timely on him:
I have almost slipp'd the hour.

MACBETH

I'll bring you to him.

MACDUFF

I know this is a joyful trouble to you;
But yet 'tis one.

MACBETH

The labour we delight in physics pain.
This is the door.

MACDUFF

I'll make so bold to call,

For 'tis my limited service.

Exit

LENNOX

Goes the king hence to-day?

MACBETH

He does: he did appoint so.

LENNOX

The night has been unruly: where we lay,

Our chimneys were blown down; and, as they
    say,

Lamentings heard i'the air; strange screams of
    death,

And prophesying with accents terrible

Of dire combustion and confused events

New hatch'd to the woeful time: the obscure
    bird

Clamour'd the livelong night: some say, the
    earth

Was feverous and did shake.

MACBETH

'Twas a rough night.

LENNOX

My young remembrance cannot parallel

A fellow to it.

Re-enter Macduff

MACDUFF

> O horror, horror, horror! Tongue nor heart
> Cannot conceive nor name thee!

MACBETH, LENNOX

> What's the matter.

MACDUFF

> Confusion now hath made his masterpiece!
> Most sacrilegious murder hath broke ope
> The Lord's anointed temple, and stole thence
> The life o'the building!

MACBETH

> What is't you say? the life?

LENNOX

> Mean you his majesty?

MACDUFF

> Approach the chamber, and destroy your sight
> With a new Gorgon: do not bid me speak;
> See, and then speak yourselves.

> > *Exeunt Macbeth and Lennox*

> Awake, awake!
> Ring the alarum-bell. Murder and treason!
> Banquo and Donalbain! Malcolm! awake!
> Shake off this downy sleep, death's counterfeit,
> And look on death itself! up, up, and see
> The great doom's image! Malcolm! Banquo!
> As from your graves rise up, and walk like
> sprites,

To countenance this horror! Ring the bell.

Bell rings

Enter Lady Macbeth

LADY MACBETH

What's the business,
That such a hideous trumpet calls to parley
The sleepers of the house? speak, speak!

MACDUFF

O gentle lady,
'Tis not for you to hear what I can speak:
The repetition, in a woman's ear,
Would murder as it fell.

Enter Banquo

O Banquo, Banquo,
Our royal master's murder'd!

LADY MACBETH

Woe, alas!
What, in our house?

BANQUO

Too cruel any where.
Dear Duff, I prithee, contradict thyself,
And say it is not so.

Re-enter Macbeth and Lennox, with Ross

MACBETH

Had I but died an hour before this chance,
I had lived a blessed time; for, from this instant,
There's nothing serious in mortality:

All is but toys: renown and grace is dead;
The wine of life is drawn, and the mere lees
Is left this vault to brag of.

Enter Malcolm and Donalbain

DONALBAIN

What is amiss?

MACBETH

You are, and do not know't:
The spring, the head, the fountain of your
blood
Is stopp'd; the very source of it is stopp'd.

MACDUFF

Your royal father's murder'd.

MALCOLM

O, by whom?

LENNOX

Those of his chamber, as it seem'd, had done 't:
Their hands and faces were an badged with
blood;
So were their daggers, which unwiped we found
Upon their pillows:
They stared, and were distracted; no man's life
Was to be trusted with them.

MACBETH

O, yet I do repent me of my fury,
That I did kill them.

MACDUFF

Wherefore did you so?

MACBETH

Who can be wise, amazed, temperate and
furious,

Loyal and neutral, in a moment? No man:

The expedition my violent love

Outrun the pauser, reason. Here lay Duncan,

His silver skin laced with his golden blood;

And his gash'd stabs look'd like a breach in
nature

For ruin's wasteful entrance: there, the
murderers,

Steep'd in the colours of their trade, their
daggers

Unmannerly breech'd with gore: who could
refrain,

That had a heart to love, and in that heart

Courage to make's love known?

LADY MACBETH

Help me hence, ho!

MACDUFF

Look to the lady.

MALCOLM

[*Aside to Donalbain*] Why do we hold our
tongues,

That most may claim this argument for ours?

DONALBAIN

[*Aside to Malcolm*] What should be spoken here,
where our fate,

Hid in an auger-hole, may rush, and seize us?
Let's away;

Our tears are not yet brew'd.

MALCOLM

[*Aside to Donalbain*] Nor our strong sorrow
Upon the foot of motion.

BANQUO

Look to the lady:

Lady Macbeth is carried out

And when we have our naked frailties hid,
That suffer in exposure, let us meet,
And question this most bloody piece of work,
To know it further. Fears and scruples shake us:
In the great hand of God I stand; and thence
Against the undivulged pretence I fight
Of treasonous malice.

MACDUFF

And so do I.

ALL

So all.

MACBETH

Let's briefly put on manly readiness,
And meet i'the hall together.

ALL

    Well contented.

               Exeunt all but Malcolm and Donalbain.

MALCOLM

    What will you do? Let's not consort with them:

    To show an unfelt sorrow is an office

    Which the false man does easy. I'll to England.

DONALBAIN

    To Ireland, I; our separated fortune

    Shall keep us both the safer: where we are,

    There's daggers in men's smiles: the near in blood,

    The nearer bloody.

MALCOLM

    This murderous shaft that's shot

    Hath not yet lighted, and our safest way

    Is to avoid the aim. Therefore, to horse;

    And let us not be dainty of leave-taking,

    But shift away: there's warrant in that theft

    Which steals itself, when there's no mercy left.

                       Exeunt

SCENE IV. OUTSIDE MACBETH'S CASTLE.

Enter Ross and an old Man

OLD MAN

    Threescore and ten I can remember well:

    Within the volume of which time I have seen

Hours dreadful and things strange; but this
    sore night
Hath trifled former knowings.

ROSS

Ah, good father,
Thou seest, the heavens, as troubled with
    man's act,
Threaten his bloody stage: by the clock, 'tis day,
And yet dark night strangles the travelling lamp:
Is't night's predominance, or the day's shame,
That darkness does the face of earth entomb,
When living light should kiss it?

OLD MAN

'Tis unnatural,
Even like the deed that's done. On Tuesday last,
A falcon, towering in her pride of place,
Was by a mousing owl hawk'd at and kill'd.

ROSS

And Duncan's horses—a thing most strange
    and certain—
Beauteous and swift, the minions of their race,
Turn'd wild in nature, broke their stalls, flung
    out,
Contending 'gainst obedience, as they would
    make
War with mankind.

OLD MAN

    'Tis said they eat each other.

ROSS

    They did so, to the amazement of mine eyes

    That look'd upon't. Here comes the good Macduff.

               Enter Macduff

    How goes the world, sir, now?

MACDUFF

    Why, see you not?

ROSS

    Is't known who did this more than bloody deed?

MACDUFF

    Those that Macbeth hath slain.

ROSS

    Alas, the day!

    What good could they pretend?

MACDUFF

    They were suborn'd:

    Malcolm and Donalbain, the king's two sons,

    Are stol'n away and fled; which puts upon them

    Suspicion of the deed.

ROSS

    'Gainst nature still!

    Thriftless ambition, that wilt ravin up

    Thine own life's means! Then 'tis most like

    The sovereignty will fall upon Macbeth.

MACDUFF

> He is already named, and gone to Scone
> To be invested.

ROSS

> Where is Duncan's body?

MACDUFF

> Carried to Colmekill,
> The sacred storehouse of his predecessors,
> And guardian of their bones.

ROSS

> Will you to Scone?

MACDUFF

> No, cousin, I'll to Fife.

ROSS

> Well, I will thither.

MACDUFF

> Well, may you see things well done there: Adieu!
> Lest our old robes sit easier than our new!

ROSS

> Farewell, father.

OLD MAN

> God's benison go with you; and with those
> That would make good of bad, and friends of
>> foes!

Exeunt

***

Act III

SCENE I. FORRES. THE PALACE.

Enter Banquo
BANQUO
    Thou hast it now: king, Cawdor, Glamis, all,
    As the weird women promised, and, I fear,
    Thou play'dst most foully for't: yet it was said
    It should not stand in thy posterity,
    But that myself should be the root and father
    Of many kings. If there come truth from
        them—
    As upon thee, Macbeth, their speeches shine—
    Why, by the verities on thee made good,
    May they not be my oracles as well,
    And set me up in hope? But hush! no more.
       Sennet sounded. Enter Macbeth, as king,
         Lady Macbeth, as queen, Lennox,
         Ross, Lords, Ladies, and Attendants

MACBETH

Here's our chief guest.

LADY MACBETH

If he had been forgotten,

It had been as a gap in our great feast,

And all-thing unbecoming.

MACBETH

To-night we hold a solemn supper sir,

And I'll request your presence.

BANQUO

Let your highness

Command upon me; to the which my duties

Are with a most indissoluble tie

For ever knit.

MACBETH

Ride you this afternoon?

BANQUO

Ay, my good lord.

MACBETH

We should have else desired your good advice,

Which still hath been both grave and

prosperous,

In this day's council; but we'll take to-morrow.

Is't far you ride?

BANQUO

As far, my lord, as will fill up the time

'Twixt this and supper: go not my horse the
    better,
I must become a borrower of the night
For a dark hour or twain.

MACBETH

Fail not our feast.

BANQUO

My lord, I will not.

MACBETH

We hear, our bloody cousins are bestow'd
In England and in Ireland, not confessing
Their cruel parricide, filling their hearers
With strange invention: but of that to-morrow,
When therewithal we shall have cause of state
Craving us jointly. Hie you to horse: Adieu,
Till you return at night. Goes Fleance with you?

BANQUO

Ay, my good lord: our time does call upon's.

MACBETH

I wish your horses swift and sure of foot;
And so I do commend you to their backs.
    Farewell.

Exit Banquo

Let every man be master of his time
Till seven at night: to make society
The sweeter welcome, we will keep ourself

Till supper-time alone: while then, God be
    with you!

Exeunt all but Macbeth, and
an attendant

Sirrah, a word with you: attend those men
Our pleasure?

ATTENDANT

They are, my lord, without the palace gate.

MACBETH

Bring them before us.

Exit Attendant

To be thus is nothing;
But to be safely thus.—Our fears in Banquo
Stick deep; and in his royalty of nature
Reigns that which would be fear'd: 'tis much
    he dares;
And, to that dauntless temper of his mind,
He hath a wisdom that doth guide his valour
To act in safety. There is none but he
Whose being I do fear: and, under him,
My Genius is rebuked; as, it is said,
Mark Antony's was by Caesar. He chid the
    sisters
When first they put the name of king upon me,
And bade them speak to him: then prophet-like
They hail'd him father to a line of kings:
Upon my head they placed a fruitless crown,

And put a barren sceptre in my gripe,
Thence to be wrench'd with an unlineal hand,
No son of mine succeeding. If 't be so,
For Banquo's issue have I filed my mind;
For them the gracious Duncan have I murder'd;
Put rancours in the vessel of my peace
Only for them; and mine eternal jewel
Given to the common enemy of man,
To make them kings, the seed of Banquo kings!
Rather than so, come fate into the list.
And champion me to the utterance! Who's there!

Re-enter Attendant, with two Murderers

Now go to the door, and stay there till we call.

Exit Attendant

Was it not yesterday we spoke together?

FIRST MURDERER

It was, so please your highness.

MACBETH

Well then, now
Have you consider'd of my speeches? Know
That it was he in the times past which held you
So under fortune, which you thought had been
Our innocent self: This I made good to you
In our last conference, pass'd in probation with
    you,
How you were borne in hand, how cross'd, the
    instruments,

69

Who wrought with them, and all things else
    that might
To half a soul and to a notion crazed
Say 'Thus did Banquo.'

FIRST MURDERER

You made it known to us.

MACBETH

I did so, and went further, which is now
Our point of second meeting. Do you find
Your patience so predominant in your nature
That you can let this go? Are you so gospell'd
To pray for this good man and for his issue,
Whose heavy hand hath bow'd you to the grave
And beggar'd yours for ever?

FIRST MURDERER

We are men, my liege.

MACBETH

Ay, in the catalogue ye go for men;
As hounds and greyhounds, mongrels, spaniels,
    curs,
Shoughs, water-rugs and demi-wolves, are clept
All by the name of dogs: the valued file
Distinguishes the swift, the slow, the subtle,
The housekeeper, the hunter, every one
According to the gift which bounteous nature
Hath in him closed; whereby he does receive
Particular addition. from the bill

That writes them all alike: and so of men.
Now, if you have a station in the file,
Not i'the worst rank of manhood, say't;
And I will put that business in your bosoms,
Whose execution takes your enemy off,
Grapples you to the heart and love of us,
Who wear our health but sickly in his life,
Which in his death were perfect.

SECOND MURDERER

I am one, my liege,
Whom the vile blows and buffets of the world
Have so incensed that I am reckless what
I do to spite the world.

FIRST MURDERER

And I another
So weary with disasters, tugg'd with fortune,
That I would set my lie on any chance,
To mend it, or be rid on't.

MACBETH

Both of you
Know Banquo was your enemy.

BOTH MURDERERS

True, my lord.

MACBETH

So is he mine; and in such bloody distance,
That every minute of his being thrusts
Against my near'st of life: and though I could

With barefaced power sweep him from my
    sight
And bid my will avouch it, yet I must not,
For certain friends that are both his and mine,
Whose loves I may not drop, but wail his fall
Who I myself struck down; and thence it is,
That I to your assistance do make love,
Masking the business from the common eye
For sundry weighty reasons.

SECOND MURDERER

We shall, my lord,
Perform what you command us.

FIRST MURDERER

Though our lives—

MACBETH

Your spirits shine through you. Within this
    hour at most
I will advise you where to plant yourselves;
Acquaint you with the perfect spy o'the time,
The moment on't; for't must be done to-night,
And something from the palace; always thought
That I require a clearness: and with him—
To leave no rubs nor botches in the work—
Fleance his son, that keeps him company,
Whose absence is no less material to me
Than is his father's, must embrace the fate

Of that dark hour. Resolve yourselves apart:

I'll come to you anon.

BOTH MURDERERS

We are resolved, my lord.

MACBETH

I'll call upon you straight: abide within.

Exeunt Murderers

It is concluded. Banquo, thy soul's flight,

If it find heaven, must find it out to-night.

Exit

SCENE II. THE PALACE.

Enter Lady Macbeth and a Servant

LADY MACBETH

Is Banquo gone from court?

SERVANT

Ay, madam, but returns again to-night.

LADY MACBETH

Say to the king, I would attend his leisure

For a few words.

SERVANT

Madam, I will.

Exit

LADY MACBETH

Nought's had, all's spent,

Where our desire is got without content:

'Tis safer to be that which we destroy
Than by destruction dwell in doubtful joy.

Enter Macbeth

How now, my lord! why do you keep alone,
Of sorriest fancies your companions making,
Using those thoughts which should indeed
    have died
With them they think on? Things without all
    remedy
Should be without regard: what's done is done.

MACBETH

We have scotch'd the snake, not kill'd it:
She'll close and be herself, whilst our poor malice
Remains in danger of her former tooth.
But let the frame of things disjoint, both the
    worlds suffer,
Ere we will eat our meal in fear and sleep
In the affliction of these terrible dreams
That shake us nightly: better be with the dead,
Whom we, to gain our peace, have sent to peace,
Than on the torture of the mind to lie
In restless ecstasy. Duncan is in his grave;
After life's fitful fever he sleeps well;
Treason has done his worst: nor steel, nor
    poison,
Malice domestic, foreign levy, nothing,
Can touch him further.

LADY MACBETH

Come on;

Gentle my lord, sleek o'er your rugged looks;

Be bright and jovial among your guests to-
night.

MACBETH

So shall I, love; and so, I pray, be you:

Let your remembrance apply to Banquo;

Present him eminence, both with eye and
tongue:

Unsafe the while, that we

Must lave our honours in these flattering
streams,

And make our faces vizards to our hearts,

Disguising what they are.

LADY MACBETH

You must leave this.

MACBETH

O, full of scorpions is my mind, dear wife!

Thou know'st that Banquo, and his Fleance, lives.

LADY MACBETH

But in them nature's copy's not eterne.

MACBETH

There's comfort yet; they are assailable;

Then be thou jocund: ere the bat hath flown

His cloister'd flight, ere to black Hecate's
summons

The shard-borne beetle with his drowsy hums
Hath rung night's yawning peal, there shall be
    done
A deed of dreadful note.

LADY MACBETH

What's to be done?

MACBETH

Be innocent of the knowledge, dearest chuck,
Till thou applaud the deed. Come, seeling night,
Scarf up the tender eye of pitiful day;
And with thy bloody and invisible hand
Cancel and tear to pieces that great bond
Which keeps me pale! Light thickens; and the
    crow
Makes wing to the rooky wood:
Good things of day begin to droop and drowse;
While night's black agents to their preys do
    rouse.
Thou marvell'st at my words: but hold thee still;
Things bad begun make strong themselves
    by ill.
So, prithee, go with me.

Exeunt

SCENE III. A PARK NEAR THE PALACE.

Enter three Murderers

FIRST MURDERER

    But who did bid thee join with us?

THIRD MURDERER

    Macbeth.

SECOND MURDERER

    He needs not our mistrust, since he delivers

    Our offices and what we have to do

    To the direction just.

FIRST MURDERER

    Then stand with us.

    The west yet glimmers with some streaks of day:

    Now spurs the lated traveller apace

    To gain the timely inn; and near approaches

    The subject of our watch.

THIRD MURDERER

    Hark! I hear horses.

BANQUO

    [*Within*] Give us a light there, ho!

SECOND MURDERER

    Then 'tis he: the rest

    That are within the note of expectation

    Already are i'the court.

FIRST MURDERER

    His horses go about.

THIRD MURDERER

Almost a mile: but he does usually,
So all men do, from hence to the palace gate
Make it their walk.

SECOND MURDERER

A light, a light!

Enter Banquo, and Fleance with a torch

THIRD MURDERER

'Tis he.

FIRST MURDERER

Stand to't.

BANQUO

It will be rain to-night.

FIRST MURDERER

Let it come down.

They set upon Banquo

BANQUO

O, treachery! Fly, good Fleance, fly, fly, fly!
Thou mayst revenge. O slave!

Dies. Fleance escapes

THIRD MURDERER

Who did strike out the light?

FIRST MURDERER

Wast not the way?

THIRD MURDERER

There's but one down; the son is fled.

SECOND MURDERER

    We have lost

    Best half of our affair.

FIRST MURDERER

    Well, let's away, and say how much is done.

Exeunt

SCENE IV. THE SAME.
HALL IN THE PALACE.

A banquet prepared. Enter Macbeth, Lady Macbeth, Ross,
Lennox, Lords, and Attendants

MACBETH

    You know your own degrees; sit down: At first

    And last the hearty welcome.

LORDS

    Thanks to your majesty.

MACBETH

    Ourself will mingle with society,

    And play the humble host.

    Our hostess keeps her state, but in best time

    We will require her welcome.

LADY MACBETH

    Pronounce it for me, sir, to all our friends;

    For my heart speaks they are welcome.

    First Murderer appears at the door

MACBETH

See, they encounter thee with their hearts'
thanks.

Both sides are even: here I'll sit i'the midst:

Be large in mirth; anon we'll drink a measure

The table round.

Approaching the door

There's blood on thy face.

FIRST MURDERER

'Tis Banquo's then.

MACBETH

'Tis better thee without than he within.

Is he dispatch'd?

FIRST MURDERER

My lord, his throat is cut; that I did for him.

MACBETH

Thou art the best o'the cut-throats: yet he's
good

That did the like for Fleance: if thou didst it,

Thou art the nonpareil.

FIRST MURDERER

Most royal sir,

Fleance is 'scaped.

MACBETH

Then comes my fit again: I had else been
perfect,

Whole as the marble, founded as the rock,
As broad and general as the casing air:
But now I am cabin'd, cribb'd, confined,
  bound in
To saucy doubts and fears. But Banquo's safe?

FIRST MURDERER

Ay, my good lord: safe in a ditch he bides,
With twenty trenched gashes on his head;
The least a death to nature.

MACBETH

Thanks for that:
There the grown serpent lies; the worm that's
  fled
Hath nature that in time will venom breed,
No teeth for the present. Get thee gone: to-
  morrow
We'll hear, ourselves, again.

Exit Murderer

LADY MACBETH

My royal lord,
You do not give the cheer: the feast is sold
That is not often vouch'd, while 'tis a-making,
'Tis given with welcome: to feed were best at
  home;
From thence the sauce to meat is ceremony;
Meeting were bare without it.

MACBETH

Sweet remembrancer!

Now, good digestion wait on appetite,

And health on both!

LENNOX

May't please your highness sit.

The Ghost Of Banquo enters, and
sits in Macbeth's place

MACBETH

Here had we now our country's honour roof'd,

Were the graced person of our Banquo present;

Who may I rather challenge for unkindness

Than pity for mischance!

ROSS

His absence, sir,

Lays blame upon his promise. Please't your
highness

To grace us with your royal company.

MACBETH

The table's full.

LENNOX

Here is a place reserved, sir.

MACBETH

Where?

LENNOX

Here, my good lord. What is't that moves your
highness?

MACBETH

>Which of you have done this?

LORDS

>What, my good lord?

MACBETH

>Thou canst not say I did it: never shake
>Thy gory locks at me.

ROSS

>Gentlemen, rise: his highness is not well.

LADY MACBETH

>Sit, worthy friends: my lord is often thus,
>And hath been from his youth: pray you, keep
>>seat;
>The fit is momentary; upon a thought
>He will again be well: if much you note him,
>You shall offend him and extend his passion:
>Feed, and regard him not. Are you a man?

MACBETH

>Ay, and a bold one, that dare look on that
>Which might appal the devil.

LADY MACBETH

>O proper stuff!
>This is the very painting of your fear:
>This is the air-drawn dagger which, you said,
>Led you to Duncan. O, these flaws and starts,
>Impostors to true fear, would well become
>A woman's story at a winter's fire,

Authorized by her grandam. Shame itself!
Why do you make such faces? When all's done,
You look but on a stool.

MACBETH

Prithee, see there! behold! look! lo! how say
you?
Why, what care I? If thou canst nod, speak too.
If charnel-houses and our graves must send
Those that we bury back, our monuments
Shall be the maws of kites.

Ghost of Banquo vanishes

LADY MACBETH

What, quite unmann'd in folly?

MACBETH

If I stand here, I saw him.

LADY MACBETH

Fie, for shame!

MACBETH

Blood hath been shed ere now, i'the olden time,
Ere human statute purged the gentle weal;
Ay, and since too, murders have been perform'd
Too terrible for the ear: the times have been,
That, when the brains were out, the man
would die,
And there an end; but now they rise again,
With twenty mortal murders on their crowns,

And push us from our stools: this is more
    strange
Than such a murder is.

LADY MACBETH

My worthy lord,
Your noble friends do lack you.

MACBETH

I do forget.
Do not muse at me, my most worthy friends,
I have a strange infirmity, which is nothing
To those that know me. Come, love and health
    to all;
Then I'll sit down. Give me some wine; fill full.
I drink to the general joy o'the whole table,
And to our dear friend Banquo, whom we miss;
Would he were here! to all, and him, we thirst,
And all to all.

LORDS

Our duties, and the pledge.

           Re-enter Ghost of Banquo

MACBETH

Avaunt! and quit my sight! let the earth hide
    thee!
Thy bones are marrowless, thy blood is cold;
Thou hast no speculation in those eyes
Which thou dost glare with!

LADY MACBETH

Think of this, good peers,

But as a thing of custom: 'tis no other;

Only it spoils the pleasure of the time.

MACBETH

What man dare, I dare:

Approach thou like the rugged Russian bear,

The arm'd rhinoceros, or the Hyrcan tiger;

Take any shape but that, and my firm nerves

Shall never tremble: or be alive again,

And dare me to the desert with thy sword;

If trembling I inhabit then, protest me

The baby of a girl. Hence, horrible shadow!

Unreal mockery, hence!

Ghost of Banquo vanishes

Why, so: being gone,

I am a man again. Pray you, sit still.

LADY MACBETH

You have displaced the mirth, broke the good

meeting,

With most admired disorder.

MACBETH

Can such things be,

And overcome us like a summer's cloud,

Without our special wonder? You make me

strange

Even to the disposition that I owe,

When now I think you can behold such sights,
And keep the natural ruby of your cheeks,
When mine is blanched with fear.

ROSS

What sights, my lord?

LADY MACBETH

I pray you, speak not; he grows worse and worse;
Question enrages him. At once, good night:
Stand not upon the order of your going,
But go at once.

LENNOX

Good night; and better health
Attend his majesty!

LADY MACBETH

A kind good night to all!

Exeunt all but Macbeth and
Lady Macbeth

MACBETH

It will have blood; they say, blood will have blood:
Stones have been known to move and trees to
speak;
Augurs and understood relations have
By magot-pies and choughs and rooks brought
forth
The secret'st man of blood. What is the night?

LADY MACBETH

Almost at odds with morning, which is which.

MACBETH

How say'st thou, that Macduff denies his person
At our great bidding?

LADY MACBETH

Did you send to him, sir?

MACBETH

I hear it by the way; but I will send:
There's not a one of them but in his house
I keep a servant fee'd. I will to-morrow,
And betimes I will, to the weird sisters:
More shall they speak; for now I am bent to
    know,
By the worst means, the worst. For mine own
    good,
All causes shall give way: I am in blood
Stepp'd in so far that, should I wade no more,
Returning were as tedious as go o'er:
Strange things I have in head, that will to hand;
Which must be acted ere they may be scann'd.

LADY MACBETH

You lack the season of all natures, sleep.

MACBETH

Come, we'll to sleep. My strange and self-abuse
Is the initiate fear that wants hard use:
We are yet but young in deed.

Exeunt

SCENE V. A HEATH.

Thunder. Enter the three Witches meeting Hecate

FIRST WITCH

    Why, how now, Hecate! you look angerly.

HECATE

    Have I not reason, beldams as you are,
    Saucy and overbold? How did you dare
    To trade and traffic with Macbeth
    In riddles and affairs of death;
    And I, the mistress of your charms,
    The close contriver of all harms,
    Was never call'd to bear my part,
    Or show the glory of our art?
    And, which is worse, all you have done
    Hath been but for a wayward son,
    Spiteful and wrathful, who, as others do,
    Loves for his own ends, not for you.
    But make amends now: get you gone,
    And at the pit of Acheron
    Meet me i'the morning: thither he
    Will come to know his destiny:
    Your vessels and your spells provide,
    Your charms and every thing beside.
    I am for the air; this night I'll spend
    Unto a dismal and a fatal end:

Great business must be wrought ere noon:
Upon the corner of the moon
There hangs a vaporous drop profound;
I'll catch it ere it come to ground:
And that distill'd by magic sleights
Shall raise such artificial sprites
As by the strength of their illusion
Shall draw him on to his confusion:
He shall spurn fate, scorn death, and bear
He hopes 'bove wisdom, grace and fear:
And you all know, security
Is mortals' chiefest enemy.

Music and a song within:
'Come away, come away,' etc.

Hark! I am call'd; my little spirit, see,
Sits in a foggy cloud, and stays for me.

Exit

FIRST WITCH

Come, let's make haste; she'll soon be back
again.

Exeunt

SCENE VI. FORRES. THE PALACE.

Enter Lennox and another Lord

LENNOX

    My former speeches have but hit your thoughts,

    Which can interpret further: only, I say,

    Things have been strangely borne. The gracious
        Duncan

    Was pitied of Macbeth: marry, he was dead:

    And the right-valiant Banquo walk'd too late;

    Whom, you may say, if't please you, Fleance kill'd,

    For Fleance fled: men must not walk too late.

    Who cannot want the thought how monstrous

    It was for Malcolm and for Donalbain

    To kill their gracious father? damned fact!

    How it did grieve Macbeth! did he not straight

    In pious rage the two delinquents tear,

    That were the slaves of drink and thralls of
        sleep?

    Was not that nobly done? Ay, and wisely too;

    For 'twould have anger'd any heart alive

    To hear the men deny't. So that, I say,

    He has borne all things well: and I do think

    That had he Duncan's sons under his key—

    As, an't please heaven, he shall not—they
        should find

    What 'twere to kill a father; so should Fleance.

But, peace! for from broad words and 'cause
    he fail'd
His presence at the tyrant's feast, I hear
Macduff lives in disgrace: sir, can you tell
Where he bestows himself?

LORD

The son of Duncan,
From whom this tyrant holds the due of birth
Lives in the English court, and is received
Of the most pious Edward with such grace
That the malevolence of fortune nothing
Takes from his high respect: thither Macduff
Is gone to pray the holy king, upon his aid
To wake Northumberland and warlike Siward:
That, by the help of these—with Him above
To ratify the work—we may again
Give to our tables meat, sleep to our nights,
Free from our feasts and banquets bloody knives,
Do faithful homage and receive free honours:
All which we pine for now: and this report
Hath so exasperate the king that he
Prepares for some attempt of war.

LENNOX

Sent he to Macduff?

LORD

He did: and with an absolute 'Sir, not I,'
The cloudy messenger turns me his back,

And hums, as who should say 'You'll rue the
    time
That clogs me with this answer.'

LENNOX

And that well might
Advise him to a caution, to hold what distance
His wisdom can provide. Some holy angel
Fly to the court of England and unfold
His message ere he come, that a swift blessing
May soon return to this our suffering country
Under a hand accursed!

LORD

I'll send my prayers with him.

Exeunt

***

Act IV

SCENE I. A CAVERN. IN THE MIDDLE, A BOILING CAULDRON.

Thunder. Enter the three Witches

FIRST WITCH

    Thrice the brinded cat hath mew'd.

SECOND WITCH

    Thrice and once the hedge-pig whined.

THIRD WITCH

    Harpier cries 'Tis time, 'tis time.

FIRST WITCH

    Round about the cauldron go;

    In the poison'd entrails throw.

    Toad, that under cold stone

    Days and nights has thirty-one

    Swelter'd venom sleeping got,

    Boil thou first i'the charmed pot.

ALL

    Double, double toil and trouble;

    Fire burn, and cauldron bubble.

SECOND WITCH

    Fillet of a fenny snake,

    In the cauldron boil and bake;

    Eye of newt and toe of frog,

    Wool of bat and tongue of dog,

    Adder's fork and blind-worm's sting,

    Lizard's leg and owlet's wing,

    For a charm of powerful trouble,

    Like a hell-broth boil and bubble.

ALL

    Double, double toil and trouble;

    Fire burn and cauldron bubble.

THIRD WITCH

    Scale of dragon, tooth of wolf,

    Witches' mummy, maw and gulf

    Of the ravin'd salt-sea shark,

    Root of hemlock digg'd i'the dark,

    Liver of blaspheming Jew,

    Gall of goat, and slips of yew

    Silver'd in the moon's eclipse,

    Nose of Turk and Tartar's lips,

    Finger of birth-strangled babe

    Ditch-deliver'd by a drab,

    Make the gruel thick and slab:

Add thereto a tiger's chaudron,

For the ingredients of our cauldron.

ALL

Double, double toil and trouble;

Fire burn and cauldron bubble.

SECOND WITCH

Cool it with a baboon's blood,

Then the charm is firm and good.

Enter Hecate to the other three Witches

HECATE

O well done! I commend your pains;

And every one shall share i'the gains;

And now about the cauldron sing,

Live elves and fairies in a ring,

Enchanting all that you put in.

Music and a song: 'Black spirits,' etc

Hecate retires

SECOND WITCH

By the pricking of my thumbs,

Something wicked this way comes.

Open, locks,

Whoever knocks!

Enter Macbeth

MACBETH

How now, you secret, black, and midnight hags!

What is't you do?

ALL

A deed without a name.

MACBETH

I conjure you, by that which you profess,

Howe'er you come to know it, answer me:

Though you untie the winds and let them fight

Against the churches; though the yesty waves

Confound and swallow navigation up;

Though bladed corn be lodged and trees blown
down;

Though castles topple on their warders' heads;

Though palaces and pyramids do slope

Their heads to their foundations; though the
treasure

Of nature's germens tumble all together,

Even till destruction sicken; answer me

To what I ask you.

FIRST WITCH

Speak.

SECOND WITCH

Demand.

THIRD WITCH

We'll answer.

FIRST WITCH

Say, if thou'dst rather hear it from our mouths,

Or from our masters?

MACBETH

 Call 'em; let me see 'em.

FIRST WITCH

 Pour in sow's blood, that hath eaten

 Her nine farrow; grease that's sweaten

 From the murderer's gibbet throw

 Into the flame.

ALL

 Come, high or low;

 Thyself and office deftly show!

  Thunder. First Apparition: an armed Head

MACBETH

 Tell me, thou unknown power—

FIRST WITCH

 He knows thy thought:

 Hear his speech, but say thou nought.

FIRST APPARITION

 Macbeth! Macbeth! Macbeth! beware Macduff;

 Beware the thane of Fife. Dismiss me. Enough.

  Descends

MACBETH

 Whate'er thou art, for thy good caution, thanks;

 Thou hast harp'd my fear aright: but one word

  more—

FIRST WITCH

 He will not be commanded: here's another,

 More potent than the first.

Thunder. Second Apparition: A bloody Child

SECOND APPARITION

Macbeth! Macbeth! Macbeth!

MACBETH

Had I three ears, I'ld hear thee.

SECOND APPARITION

Be bloody, bold, and resolute; laugh to scorn
The power of man, for none of woman born
Shall harm Macbeth.

Descends

MACBETH

Then live, Macduff: what need I fear of thee?
But yet I'll make assurance double sure,
And take a bond of fate: thou shalt not live;
That I may tell pale-hearted fear it lies,
And sleep in spite of thunder.

Thunder. Third Apparition: a Child crowned,
with a tree in his hand

What is this
That rises like the issue of a king,
And wears upon his baby-brow the round
And top of sovereignty?

ALL

Listen, but speak not to't.

THIRD APPARITION

Be lion-mettled, proud; and take no care
Who chafes, who frets, or where conspirers are:

Macbeth shall never vanquish'd be until
Great Birnam wood to high Dunsinane hill
Shall come against him.

Descends

MACBETH

That will never be
Who can impress the forest, bid the tree
Unfix his earth-bound root? Sweet bodements!
    good!
Rebellion's head, rise never till the wood
Of Birnam rise, and our high-placed Macbeth
Shall live the lease of nature, pay his breath
To time and mortal custom. Yet my heart
Throbs to know one thing: tell me, if your art
Can tell so much: shall Banquo's issue ever
Reign in this kingdom?

ALL

Seek to know no more.

MACBETH

I will be satisfied: deny me this,
And an eternal curse fall on you! Let me know.
Why sinks that cauldron? and what noise is this?

Hautboys

FIRST WITCH

Show!

SECOND WITCH

Show!

THIRD WITCH

Show!

ALL

Show his eyes, and grieve his heart;
Come like shadows, so depart!

*A show of Eight Kings, the last with a glass in
his hand; Ghost of Banquo following*

MACBETH

Thou art too like the spirit of Banquo: down!
Thy crown does sear mine eye-balls. And thy hair,
Thou other gold-bound brow, is like the first.
A third is like the former. Filthy hags!
Why do you show me this? A fourth! Start, eyes!
What, will the line stretch out to the crack of
    doom?
Another yet! A seventh! I'll see no more:
And yet the eighth appears, who bears a glass
Which shows me many more; and some I see
That two-fold balls and treble scepters carry:
Horrible sight! Now, I see, 'tis true;
For the blood-bolter'd Banquo smiles upon me,
And points at them for his.

Apparitions vanish

What, is this so?

FIRST WITCH

Ay, sir, all this is so: but why
Stands Macbeth thus amazedly?

Come, sisters, cheer we up his sprites,
And show the best of our delights:
I'll charm the air to give a sound,
While you perform your antic round:
That this great king may kindly say,
Our duties did his welcome pay.

*Music. The witches dance and then vanish, with
Hecate*

MACBETH

Where are they? Gone? Let this pernicious hour
Stand aye accursed in the calendar!
Come in, without there!

Enter Lennox

LENNOX

What's your grace's will?

MACBETH

Saw you the weird sisters?

LENNOX

No, my lord.

MACBETH

Came they not by you?

LENNOX

No, indeed, my lord.

MACBETH

Infected be the air whereon they ride;
And damn'd all those that trust them! I did hear
The galloping of horse: who was't came by?

LENNOX

'Tis two or three, my lord, that bring you word
Macduff is fled to England.

MACBETH

Fled to England!

LENNOX

Ay, my good lord.

MACBETH

Time, thou anticipatest my dread exploits:
The flighty purpose never is o'ertook
Unless the deed go with it; from this moment
The very firstlings of my heart shall be
The firstlings of my hand. And even now,
To crown my thoughts with acts, be it thought
    and done:
The castle of Macduff I will surprise;
Seize upon Fife; give to the edge o'the sword
His wife, his babes, and all unfortunate souls
That trace him in his line. No boasting like a
    fool;
This deed I'll do before this purpose cool.
But no more sights!—Where are these
    gentlemen?
Come, bring me where they are.

Exeunt

SCENE II. FIFE. MACDUFF'S CASTLE.

Enter Lady Macduff, her Son, and Ross

LADY MACDUFF

What had he done, to make him fly the land?

ROSS

You must have patience, madam.

LADY MACDUFF

He had none:

His flight was madness: when our actions do
     not,

Our fears do make us traitors.

ROSS

You know not

Whether it was his wisdom or his fear.

LADY MACDUFF

Wisdom! to leave his wife, to leave his babes,

His mansion and his titles in a place

From whence himself does fly? He loves us
     not;

He wants the natural touch: for the poor wren,

The most diminutive of birds, will fight,

Her young ones in her nest, against the owl.

All is the fear and nothing is the love;

As little is the wisdom, where the flight

So runs against all reason.

ROSS

My dearest coz,

I pray you, school yourself: but for your husband,

He is noble, wise, judicious, and best knows

The fits o'the season. I dare not speak much
further;

But cruel are the times, when we are traitors

And do not know ourselves, when we hold
rumour

From what we fear, yet know not what we fear,

But float upon a wild and violent sea

Each way and move. I take my leave of you:

Shall not be long but I'll be here again:

Things at the worst will cease, or else climb
upward

To what they were before. My pretty cousin,

Blessing upon you!

LADY MACDUFF

Father'd he is, and yet he's fatherless.

ROSS

I am so much a fool, should I stay longer,

It would be my disgrace and your discomfort:

I take my leave at once.

Exit

LADY MACDUFF

Sirrah, your father's dead;

And what will you do now? How will you live?

SON

As birds do, mother.

LADY MACDUFF

What, with worms and flies?

SON

With what I get, I mean; and so do they.

LADY MACDUFF

Poor bird! thou'ldst never fear the net nor lime,
The pitfall nor the gin.

SON

Why should I, mother? Poor birds they are not
    set for.
My father is not dead, for all your saying.

LADY MACDUFF

Yes, he is dead; how wilt thou do for a father?

SON

Nay, how will you do for a husband?

LADY MACDUFF

Why, I can buy me twenty at any market.

SON

Then you'll buy 'em to sell again.

LADY MACDUFF

Thou speak'st with all thy wit: and yet, i'faith,
With wit enough for thee.

SON

Was my father a traitor, mother?

LADY MACDUFF

Ay, that he was.

SON

What is a traitor?

LADY MACDUFF

Why, one that swears and lies.

SON

And be all traitors that do so?

LADY MACDUFF

Every one that does so is a traitor, and must be hanged.

SON

And must they all be hanged that swear and lie?

LADY MACDUFF

Every one.

SON

Who must hang them?

LADY MACDUFF

Why, the honest men.

SON

Then the liars and swearers are fools, for there are liars and swearers enow to beat the honest men and hang up them.

LADY MACDUFF

Now, God help thee, poor monkey! But how wilt thou do for a father?

SON

If he were dead, you'd weep for him: if you
would not, it were a good sign that I should
quickly have a new father.

LADY MACDUFF

Poor prattler, how thou talk'st!

Enter a Messenger

MESSENGER

Bless you, fair dame! I am not to you known,
Though in your state of honour I am perfect.
I doubt some danger does approach you nearly:
If you will take a homely man's advice,
Be not found here; hence, with your little ones.
To fright you thus, methinks, I am too savage;
To do worse to you were fell cruelty,
Which is too nigh your person. Heaven
    preserve you!
I dare abide no longer.

Exit

LADY MACDUFF

Whither should I fly?
I have done no harm. But I remember now
I am in this earthly world; where to do harm
Is often laudable, to do good sometime
Accounted dangerous folly: why then, alas,
Do I put up that womanly defence,

To say I have done no harm?

Enter Murderers

What are these faces?

FIRST MURDERER

Where is your husband?

LADY MACDUFF

I hope, in no place so unsanctified
Where such as thou mayst find him.

FIRST MURDERER

He's a traitor.

SON

Thou liest, thou shag-hair'd villain!

FIRST MURDERER

What, you egg!

Stabbing him

Young fry of treachery!

SON

He has kill'd me, mother:
Run away, I pray you!

Dies

Exit Lady Macduff, crying 'Murder!'
Exeunt Murderers, following her

SCENE III. ENGLAND. BEFORE THE KING'S PALACE.

Enter Malcolm and Macduff

MALCOLM

Let us seek out some desolate shade, and there
Weep our sad bosoms empty.

MACDUFF

Let us rather
Hold fast the mortal sword, and like good men
Bestride our down-fall'n birthdom: each new morn
New widows howl, new orphans cry, new sorrows
Strike heaven on the face, that it resounds
As if it felt with Scotland and yell'd out
Like syllable of dolour.

MALCOLM

What I believe I'll wail,
What know believe, and what I can redress,
As I shall find the time to friend, I will.
What you have spoke, it may be so perchance.
This tyrant, whose sole name blisters our tongues,
Was once thought honest: you have loved him well.
He hath not touch'd you yet. I am young; but something

You may deserve of him through me, and
    wisdom
To offer up a weak poor innocent lamb
To appease an angry god.

MACDUFF

    I am not treacherous.

MALCOLM

    But Macbeth is.
    A good and virtuous nature may recoil
    In an imperial charge. But I shall crave your
        pardon;
    That which you are my thoughts cannot
        transpose:
    Angels are bright still, though the brightest fell;
    Though all things foul would wear the brows
        of grace,
    Yet grace must still look so.

MACDUFF

    I have lost my hopes.

MALCOLM

    Perchance even there where I did find my
        doubts.
    Why in that rawness left you wife and child,
    Those precious motives, those strong knots of
        love,
    Without leave-taking? I pray you,
    Let not my jealousies be your dishonours,

But mine own safeties. You may be rightly just,
Whatever I shall think.

MACDUFF

Bleed, bleed, poor country!
Great tyranny! lay thou thy basis sure,
For goodness dare not cheque thee: wear thou
    thy wrongs;
The title is affeer'd! Fare thee well, lord:
I would not be the villain that thou think'st
For the whole space that's in the tyrant's grasp,
And the rich East to boot.

MALCOLM

Be not offended:
I speak not as in absolute fear of you.
I think our country sinks beneath the yoke;
It weeps, it bleeds; and each new day a gash
Is added to her wounds: I think withal
There would be hands uplifted in my right;
And here from gracious England have I offer
Of goodly thousands: but, for all this,
When I shall tread upon the tyrant's head,
Or wear it on my sword, yet my poor country
Shall have more vices than it had before,
More suffer and more sundry ways than ever,
By him that shall succeed.

MACDUFF

What should he be?

MALCOLM

>It is myself I mean: in whom I know
>All the particulars of vice so grafted
>That, when they shall be open'd, black Macbeth
>Will seem as pure as snow, and the poor state
>Esteem him as a lamb, being compared
>With my confineless harms.

MACDUFF

>Not in the legions
>Of horrid hell can come a devil more damn'd
>In evils to top Macbeth.

MALCOLM

>I grant him bloody,
>Luxurious, avaricious, false, deceitful,
>Sudden, malicious, smacking of every sin
>That has a name: but there's no bottom, none,
>In my voluptuousness: your wives, your
>   daughters,
>Your matrons and your maids, could not fill up
>The cistern of my lust, and my desire
>All continent impediments would o'erbear
>That did oppose my will: better Macbeth
>Than such an one to reign.

MACDUFF

>Boundless intemperance
>In nature is a tyranny; it hath been
>The untimely emptying of the happy throne

And fall of many kings. But fear not yet
To take upon you what is yours: you may
Convey your pleasures in a spacious plenty,
And yet seem cold, the time you may so
    hoodwink.
We have willing dames enough: there cannot be
That vulture in you, to devour so many
As will to greatness dedicate themselves,
Finding it so inclined.

MALCOLM

With this there grows
In my most ill-composed affection such
A stanchless avarice that, were I king,
I should cut off the nobles for their lands,
Desire his jewels and this other's house:
And my more-having would be as a sauce
To make me hunger more; that I should forge
Quarrels unjust against the good and loyal,
Destroying them for wealth.

MACDUFF

This avarice
Sticks deeper, grows with more pernicious root
Than summer-seeming lust, and it hath been
The sword of our slain kings: yet do not fear;
Scotland hath foisons to fill up your will.
Of your mere own: all these are portable,
With other graces weigh'd.

MALCOLM

    But I have none: the king-becoming graces,
    As justice, verity, temperance, stableness,
    Bounty, perseverance, mercy, lowliness,
    Devotion, patience, courage, fortitude,
    I have no relish of them, but abound
    In the division of each several crime,
    Acting it many ways. Nay, had I power, I should
    Pour the sweet milk of concord into hell,
    Uproar the universal peace, confound
    All unity on earth.

MACDUFF

    O Scotland, Scotland!

MALCOLM

    If such a one be fit to govern, speak:
    I am as I have spoken.

MACDUFF

    Fit to govern!
    No, not to live. O nation miserable,
    With an untitled tyrant bloody-scepter'd,
    When shalt thou see thy wholesome days again,
    Since that the truest issue of thy throne
    By his own interdiction stands accursed,
    And does blaspheme his breed? Thy royal
        father
    Was a most sainted king: the queen that bore
        thee,

Oftener upon her knees than on her feet,
Died every day she lived. Fare thee well!
These evils thou repeat'st upon thyself
Have banish'd me from Scotland. O my breast,
Thy hope ends here!

MALCOLM

Macduff, this noble passion,
Child of integrity, hath from my soul
Wiped the black scruples, reconciled my
    thoughts
To thy good truth and honour. Devilish
    Macbeth
By many of these trains hath sought to win me
Into his power, and modest wisdom plucks me
From over-credulous haste: but God above
Deal between thee and me! for even now
I put myself to thy direction, and
Unspeak mine own detraction, here abjure
The taints and blames I laid upon myself,
For strangers to my nature. I am yet
Unknown to woman, never was forsworn,
Scarcely have coveted what was mine own,
At no time broke my faith, would not betray
The devil to his fellow and delight
No less in truth than life: my first false speaking
Was this upon myself: what I am truly,
Is thine and my poor country's to command:

Whither indeed, before thy here-approach,
Old Siward, with ten thousand warlike men,
Already at a point, was setting forth.
Now we'll together; and the chance of goodness
Be like our warranted quarrel! Why are you
     silent?

MACDUFF

Such welcome and unwelcome things at once
'Tis hard to reconcile.

Enter a Doctor

MALCOLM

Well; more anon.—Comes the king forth, I
pray you?

DOCTOR

Ay, sir; there are a crew of wretched souls
That stay his cure: their malady convinces
The great assay of art; but at his touch—
Such sanctity hath heaven given his hand—
They presently amend.

MALCOLM

I thank you, doctor.

Exit Doctor

MACDUFF

What's the disease he means?

MALCOLM

'Tis call'd the evil:
A most miraculous work in this good king;

Which often, since my here-remain in England,
I have seen him do. How he solicits heaven,
Himself best knows: but strangely-visited people,
All swoln and ulcerous, pitiful to the eye,
The mere despair of surgery, he cures,
Hanging a golden stamp about their necks,
Put on with holy prayers: and 'tis spoken,
To the succeeding royalty he leaves
The healing benediction. With this strange
    virtue,
He hath a heavenly gift of prophecy,
And sundry blessings hang about his throne,
That speak him full of grace.

Enter Ross

MACDUFF

See, who comes here?

MALCOLM

My countryman; but yet I know him not.

MACDUFF

My ever-gentle cousin, welcome hither.

MALCOLM

I know him now. Good God, betimes remove
The means that makes us strangers!

ROSS

Sir, amen.

MACDUFF

Stands Scotland where it did?

ROSS

Alas, poor country!

Almost afraid to know itself. It cannot

Be call'd our mother, but our grave; where
nothing,

But who knows nothing, is once seen to smile;

Where sighs and groans and shrieks that rend
the air

Are made, not mark'd; where violent sorrow
seems

A modern ecstasy; the dead man's knell

Is there scarce ask'd for who; and good men's
lives

Expire before the flowers in their caps,

Dying or ere they sicken.

MACDUFF

O, relation

Too nice, and yet too true!

MALCOLM

What's the newest grief?

ROSS

That of an hour's age doth hiss the speaker:

Each minute teems a new one.

MACDUFF

How does my wife?

ROSS

Why, well.

MACDUFF

And all my children?

ROSS

Well too.

MACDUFF

The tyrant has not batter'd at their peace?

ROSS

No; they were well at peace when I did leave
'em.

MACDUFF

But not a niggard of your speech: how goes't?

ROSS

When I came hither to transport the tidings,
Which I have heavily borne, there ran a rumour
Of many worthy fellows that were out;
Which was to my belief witness'd the rather,
For that I saw the tyrant's power a-foot:
Now is the time of help; your eye in Scotland
Would create soldiers, make our women fight,
To doff their dire distresses.

MALCOLM

Be't their comfort
We are coming thither: gracious England hath
Lent us good Siward and ten thousand men;
An older and a better soldier none
That Christendom gives out.

ROSS

Would I could answer

This comfort with the like! But I have words

That would be howl'd out in the desert air,

Where hearing should not latch them.

MACDUFF

What concern they?

The general cause? or is it a fee-grief

Due to some single breast?

ROSS

No mind that's honest

But in it shares some woe; though the main part

Pertains to you alone.

MACDUFF

If it be mine,

Keep it not from me, quickly let me have it.

ROSS

Let not your ears despise my tongue for ever,

Which shall possess them with the heaviest sound

That ever yet they heard.

MACDUFF

Hum! I guess at it.

ROSS

Your castle is surprised; your wife and babes

Savagely slaughter'd: to relate the manner,

Were, on the quarry of these murder'd deer,

To add the death of you.

MALCOLM

Merciful heaven!

What, man! Ne'er pull your hat upon your brows;

Give sorrow words: the grief that does not speak

Whispers the o'er-fraught heart and bids it break.

MACDUFF

My children too?

ROSS

Wife, children, servants, all

That could be found.

MACDUFF

And I must be from thence!

My wife kill'd too?

ROSS

I have said.

MALCOLM

Be comforted:

Let's make us medicines of our great revenge,

To cure this deadly grief.

MACDUFF

He has no children. All my pretty ones?

Did you say all? O hell-kite! All?

What, all my pretty chickens and their dam

At one fell swoop?

MALCOLM

Dispute it like a man.

MACDUFF

I shall do so;

But I must also feel it as a man:

I cannot but remember such things were,

That were most precious to me. Did heaven
look on,

And would not take their part? Sinful Macduff,

They were all struck for thee! naught that I am,

Not for their own demerits, but for mine,

Fell slaughter on their souls. Heaven rest them
now!

MALCOLM

Be this the whetstone of your sword: let grief

Convert to anger; blunt not the heart, enrage it.

MACDUFF

O, I could play the woman with mine eyes

And braggart with my tongue! But, gentle
heavens,

Cut short all intermission; front to front

Bring thou this fiend of Scotland and myself;

Within my sword's length set him; if he 'scape,

Heaven forgive him too!

MALCOLM

This tune goes manly.

Come, go we to the king; our power is ready;

Our lack is nothing but our leave; Macbeth
Is ripe for shaking, and the powers above
Put on their instruments. Receive what cheer
    you may:
The night is long that never finds the day.

                                          Exeunt

                    ***

Act V

SCENE I. DUNSINANE.
ANTE-ROOM IN THE CASTLE.

Enter a Doctor of Physic and a Waiting-Gentlewoman

DOCTOR

I have two nights watched with you, but can perceive no truth in your report. When was it she last walked?

GENTLEWOMAN

Since his majesty went into the field, I have seen her rise from her bed, throw her night-gown upon her, unlock her closet, take forth paper, fold it, write upon't, read it, afterwards seal it, and again return to bed; yet all this while in a most fast sleep.

DOCTOR

A great perturbation in nature, to receive at once the benefit of sleep, and do the effects of watching! In this slumbery agitation, besides her walking and other actual performances, what, at any time, have you heard her say?

GENTLEWOMAN

That, sir, which I will not report after her.

DOCTOR

You may to me: and 'tis most meet you should.

GENTLEWOMAN

Neither to you nor any one; having no witness to confirm my speech.

Enter Lady Macbeth, with a taper

Lo you, here she comes! This is her very guise; and, upon my life, fast asleep. Observe her; stand close.

DOCTOR

How came she by that light?

GENTLEWOMAN

Why, it stood by her: she has light by her continually; 'tis her command.

DOCTOR

You see, her eyes are open.

GENTLEWOMAN

Ay, but their sense is shut.

DOCTOR

What is it she does now? Look, how she rubs her hands.

GENTLEWOMAN

It is an accustomed action with her, to seem thus washing her hands: I have known her continue in this a quarter of an hour.

LADY MACBETH

Yet here's a spot.

DOCTOR

Hark! she speaks: I will set down what comes from her, to satisfy my remembrance the more strongly.

LADY MACBETH

Out, damned spot! out, I say!—One: two: why, then, 'tis time to do't.—Hell is murky!— Fie, my lord, fie! a soldier, and afeard? What need we fear who knows it, when none can call our power to account?—Yet who would have thought the old man to have had so much blood in him.

DOCTOR

Do you mark that?

LADY MACBETH

The thane of Fife had a wife: where is she now?—What, will these hands ne'er be clean?— No more o' that, my lord, no more o'that: you mar all with this starting.

DOCTOR

Go to, go to; you have known what you should
not.

GENTLEWOMAN

She has spoke what she should not, I am sure of
that: heaven knows what she has known.

LADY MACBETH

Here's the smell of the blood still: all the
perfumes of Arabia will not sweeten this little
hand. Oh, oh, oh!

DOCTOR

What a sigh is there! The heart is sorely charged.

GENTLEWOMAN

I would not have such a heart in my bosom for
the dignity of the whole body.

DOCTOR

Well, well, well—

GENTLEWOMAN

Pray God it be, sir.

DOCTOR

This disease is beyond my practise: yet I have
known those which have walked in their sleep
who have died holily in their beds.

LADY MACBETH

Wash your hands, put on your nightgown; look
not so pale.—I tell you yet again, Banquo's
buried; he cannot come out on's grave.

DOCTOR

Even so?

LADY MACBETH

To bed, to bed! there's knocking at the gate:
come, come, come, come, give me your hand.
What's done cannot be undone.—To bed, to
bed, to bed!

Exit

DOCTOR

Will she go now to bed?

GENTLEWOMAN

Directly.

DOCTOR

Foul whisperings are abroad: unnatural deeds
Do breed unnatural troubles: infected minds
To their deaf pillows will discharge their secrets:
More needs she the divine than the physician.
God, God forgive us all! Look after her;
Remove from her the means of all annoyance,
And still keep eyes upon her. So, good night:
My mind she has mated, and amazed my sight.
I think, but dare not speak.

GENTLEWOMAN

Good night, good doctor.

Exeunt

SCENE II. THE COUNTRY
NEAR DUNSINANE.

Drum and colours. Enter Menteith, Caithness, Angus,
Lennox, and Soldiers

MENTEITH

    The English power is near, led on by Malcolm,

    His uncle Siward and the good Macduff:

    Revenges burn in them; for their dear causes

    Would to the bleeding and the grim alarm

    Excite the mortified man.

ANGUS

    Near Birnam wood

    Shall we well meet them; that way are they coming.

CAITHNESS

    Who knows if Donalbain be with his brother?

LENNOX

    For certain, sir, he is not: I have a file

    Of all the gentry: there is Siward's son,

    And many unrough youths that even now

    Protest their first of manhood.

MENTEITH

    What does the tyrant?

CAITHNESS

    Great Dunsinane he strongly fortifies:

    Some say he's mad; others that lesser hate him

    Do call it valiant fury: but, for certain,

He cannot buckle his distemper'd cause
Within the belt of rule.

ANGUS

Now does he feel
His secret murders sticking on his hands;
Now minutely revolts upbraid his faith-breach;
Those he commands move only in command,
Nothing in love: now does he feel his title
Hang loose about him, like a giant's robe
Upon a dwarfish thief.

MENTEITH

Who then shall blame
His pester'd senses to recoil and start,
When all that is within him does condemn
Itself for being there?

CAITHNESS

Well, march we on,
To give obedience where 'tis truly owed:
Meet we the medicine of the sickly weal,
And with him pour we in our country's purge
Each drop of us.

LENNOX

Or so much as it needs,
To dew the sovereign flower and drown the
weeds.
Make we our march towards Birnam.

Exeunt, marching

SCENE III. DUNSINANE.
A ROOM IN THE CASTLE.

Enter Macbeth, Doctor, and Attendants

MACBETH

Bring me no more reports; let them fly all:

Till Birnam wood remove to Dunsinane,

I cannot taint with fear. What's the boy Malcolm?

Was he not born of woman? The spirits that know

All mortal consequences have pronounced me thus:

'Fear not, Macbeth; no man that's born of woman

Shall e'er have power upon thee.' Then fly, false thanes,

And mingle with the English epicures:

The mind I sway by and the heart I bear

Shall never sag with doubt nor shake with fear.

Enter a Servant

The devil damn thee black, thou cream-faced loon!

Where got'st thou that goose look?

SERVANT

There is ten thousand—

MACBETH

Geese, villain!

SERVANT

Soldiers, sir.

MACBETH

Go prick thy face, and over-red thy fear,

Thou lily-liver'd boy. What soldiers, patch?

Death of thy soul! those linen cheeks of thine

Are counsellors to fear. What soldiers, whey-
face?

SERVANT

The English force, so please you.

MACBETH

Take thy face hence.

Exit Servant

Seyton!—I am sick at heart,

When I behold—Seyton, I say!—This push

Will cheer me ever, or disseat me now.

I have lived long enough: my way of life

Is fall'n into the sear, the yellow leaf;

And that which should accompany old age,

As honour, love, obedience, troops of friends,

I must not look to have; but, in their stead,

Curses, not loud but deep, mouth-honour,
breath,

Which the poor heart would fain deny, and dare
not. Seyton!

Enter Seyton

SEYTON

    What is your gracious pleasure?

MACBETH

    What news more?

SEYTON

    All is confirm'd, my lord, which was reported.

MACBETH

    I'll fight till from my bones my flesh be hack'd.

    Give me my armour.

SEYTON

    'Tis not needed yet.

MACBETH

    I'll put it on.

    Send out more horses; skirr the country round;

    Hang those that talk of fear. Give me mine
        armour.

    How does your patient, doctor?

DOCTOR

    Not so sick, my lord,

    As she is troubled with thick coming fancies,

    That keep her from her rest.

MACBETH

    Cure her of that.

    Canst thou not minister to a mind diseased,

    Pluck from the memory a rooted sorrow,

Raze out the written troubles of the brain
And with some sweet oblivious antidote
Cleanse the stuff'd bosom of that perilous stuff
Which weighs upon the heart?

DOCTOR

Therein the patient
Must minister to himself.

MACBETH

Throw physic to the dogs; I'll none of it.
Come, put mine armour on; give me my staff.
Seyton, send out. Doctor, the thanes fly from me.
Come, sir, dispatch. If thou couldst, doctor, cast
The water of my land, find her disease,
And purge it to a sound and pristine health,
I would applaud thee to the very echo,
That should applaud again.—Pull't off, I say.—
What rhubarb, cyme, or what purgative drug,
Would scour these English hence? Hear'st thou
    of them?

DOCTOR

Ay, my good lord; your royal preparation
Makes us hear something.

MACBETH

Bring it after me.
I will not be afraid of death and bane,
Till Birnam forest come to Dunsinane.

DOCTOR

    [*Aside*] Were I from Dunsinane away and clear,

    Profit again should hardly draw me here.

Exeunt

SCENE IV. COUNTRY NEAR BIRNAM WOOD.

Drum and colours. Enter Malcolm, Siward and Young Siward, Macduff, Menteith, Caithness, Angus, Lennox, Ross, and Soldiers, marching

MALCOLM

    Cousins, I hope the days are near at hand

    That chambers will be safe.

MENTEITH

    We doubt it nothing.

SIWARD

    What wood is this before us?

MENTEITH

    The wood of Birnam.

MALCOLM

    Let every soldier hew him down a bough

    And bear't before him: thereby shall we shadow

    The numbers of our host and make discovery

    Err in report of us.

SOLDIERS

    It shall be done.

SIWARD

>We learn no other but the confident tyrant
>Keeps still in Dunsinane, and will endure
>Our setting down before't.

MALCOLM

>'Tis his main hope:
>For where there is advantage to be given,
>Both more and less have given him the revolt,
>And none serve with him but constrained
>>things
>Whose hearts are absent too.

MACDUFF

>Let our just censures
>Attend the true event, and put we on
>Industrious soldiership.

SIWARD

>The time approaches
>That will with due decision make us know
>What we shall say we have and what we owe.
>Thoughts speculative their unsure hopes relate,
>But certain issue strokes must arbitrate:
>Towards which advance the war.

>>>>*Exeunt, marching*

SCENE V. DUNSINANE.
WITHIN THE CASTLE.

Enter Macbeth, Seyton, and Soldiers, with drum and colours

MACBETH

    Hang out our banners on the outward walls;

    The cry is still 'They come:' our castle's strength

    Will laugh a siege to scorn: here let them lie

    Till famine and the ague eat them up:

    Were they not forced with those that should be
        ours,

    We might have met them dareful, beard to
        beard,

    And beat them backward home.

              A cry of women within

    What is that noise?

SEYTON

    It is the cry of women, my good lord.

                       Exit

MACBETH

    I have almost forgot the taste of fears;

    The time has been, my senses would have cool'd

    To hear a night-shriek; and my fell of hair

    Would at a dismal treatise rouse and stir

    As life were in't: I have supp'd full with horrors;

    Direness, familiar to my slaughterous thoughts

    Cannot once start me.

Re-enter Seyton

Wherefore was that cry?

SEYTON

The queen, my lord, is dead.

MACBETH

She should have died hereafter;
There would have been a time for such a word.
To-morrow, and to-morrow, and to-morrow,
Creeps in this petty pace from day to day
To the last syllable of recorded time,
And all our yesterdays have lighted fools
The way to dusty death. Out, out, brief candle!
Life's but a walking shadow, a poor player
That struts and frets his hour upon the stage
And then is heard no more: it is a tale
Told by an idiot, full of sound and fury,
Signifying nothing.

Enter a Messenger

Thou comest to use thy tongue; thy story
quickly.

MESSENGER

Gracious my lord,
I should report that which I say I saw,
But know not how to do it.

MACBETH

Well, say, sir.

MESSENGER

    As I did stand my watch upon the hill,
    I look'd toward Birnam, and anon, methought,
    The wood began to move.

MACBETH

    Liar and slave!

MESSENGER

    Let me endure your wrath, if't be not so:
    Within this three mile may you see it coming;
    I say, a moving grove.

MACBETH

    If thou speak'st false,
    Upon the next tree shalt thou hang alive,
    Till famine cling thee: if thy speech be sooth,
    I care not if thou dost for me as much.
    I pull in resolution, and begin
    To doubt the equivocation of the fiend
    That lies like truth: 'Fear not, till Birnam wood
    Do come to Dunsinane:' and now a wood
    Comes toward Dunsinane. Arm, arm, and out!
    If this which he avouches does appear,
    There is nor flying hence nor tarrying here.
    I gin to be aweary of the sun,
    And wish the estate o'the world were now undone.
    Ring the alarum-bell! Blow, wind! come, wrack!
    At least we'll die with harness on our back.

Exeunt

SCENE VI. DUNSINANE.
BEFORE THE CASTLE.

Drum and colours. Enter Malcolm, Siward, Macduff, and their Army, with boughs

MALCOLM

Now near enough: your leafy screens throw down.

And show like those you are. You, worthy uncle,

Shall, with my cousin, your right-noble son,

Lead our first battle: worthy Macduff and we

Shall take upon's what else remains to do,

According to our order.

SIWARD

Fare you well.

Do we but find the tyrant's power to-night,

Let us be beaten, if we cannot fight.

MACDUFF

Make all our trumpets speak; give them all breath,

Those clamorous harbingers of blood and death.

Exeunt

SCENE VII. ANOTHER PART OF THE FIELD.

Alarums. Enter Macbeth

MACBETH

They have tied me to a stake; I cannot fly,
But, bear-like, I must fight the course. What's he
That was not born of woman? Such a one
Am I to fear, or none.

Enter Young Siward

YOUNG SIWARD

What is thy name?

MACBETH

Thou'lt be afraid to hear it.

YOUNG SIWARD

No; though thou call'st thyself a hotter name
Than any is in hell.

MACBETH

My name's Macbeth.

YOUNG SIWARD

The devil himself could not pronounce a title
More hateful to mine ear.

MACBETH

No, nor more fearful.

YOUNG SIWARD

Thou liest, abhorred tyrant; with my sword
I'll prove the lie thou speak'st.

They fight and Young Siward is slain

MACBETH

    Thou wast born of woman

    But swords I smile at, weapons laugh to scorn,

    Brandish'd by man that's of a woman born.

                              Exit

Alarums. Enter Macduff

MACDUFF

    That way the noise is. Tyrant, show thy face!

    If thou be'st slain and with no stroke of mine,

    My wife and children's ghosts will haunt me
        still.

    I cannot strike at wretched kerns, whose arms

    Are hired to bear their staves: either thou,
        Macbeth,

    Or else my sword with an unbatter'd edge

    I sheathe again undeeded. There thou shouldst
        be;

    By this great clatter, one of greatest note

    Seems bruited. Let me find him, fortune!

    And more I beg not.

                              Exit.

Alarums. Enter Malcolm and Siward

SIWARD

    This way, my lord; the castle's gently render'd:

    The tyrant's people on both sides do fight;

    The noble thanes do bravely in the war;

The day almost itself professes yours,
And little is to do.

MALCOLM

We have met with foes
That strike beside us.

SIWARD

Enter, sir, the castle.

Exeunt. Alarums

SCENE VIII. ANOTHER PART OF THE FIELD.

Enter Macbeth

MACBETH

Why should I play the Roman fool, and die
On mine own sword? whiles I see lives, the gashes
Do better upon them.

Enter Macduff

MACDUFF

Turn, hell-hound, turn!

MACBETH

Of all men else I have avoided thee:
But get thee back; my soul is too much charged
With blood of thine already.

MACDUFF

I have no words:

My voice is in my sword: thou bloodier villain
Than terms can give thee out!

They fight

MACBETH

Thou losest labour:
As easy mayst thou the intrenchant air
With thy keen sword impress as make me bleed:
Let fall thy blade on vulnerable crests;
I bear a charmed life, which must not yield,
To one of woman born.

MACDUFF

Despair thy charm;
And let the angel whom thou still hast served
Tell thee, Macduff was from his mother's
womb
Untimely ripp'd.

MACBETH

Accursed be that tongue that tells me so,
For it hath cow'd my better part of man!
And be these juggling fiends no more believed,
That palter with us in a double sense;
That keep the word of promise to our ear,
And break it to our hope. I'll not fight with
thee.

MACDUFF

Then yield thee, coward,
And live to be the show and gaze o'the time:

We'll have thee, as our rarer monsters are,
Painted on a pole, and underwrit,
'Here may you see the tyrant.'

MACBETH

I will not yield,
To kiss the ground before young Malcolm's
feet,
And to be baited with the rabble's curse.
Though Birnam wood be come to Dunsinane,
And thou opposed, being of no woman born,
Yet I will try the last. Before my body
I throw my warlike shield. Lay on, Macduff,
And damn'd be him that first cries, 'Hold,
enough!'

Exeunt, fighting. Alarums
Retreat. Flourish. Enter,
with drum and colours,
Malcolm, Siward, Ross,
the other Thanes, and Soldiers

MALCOLM

I would the friends we miss were safe arrived.

SIWARD

Some must go off: and yet, by these I see,
So great a day as this is cheaply bought.

MALCOLM

Macduff is missing, and your noble son.

ROSS

Your son, my lord, has paid a soldier's debt:
He only lived but till he was a man;
The which no sooner had his prowess confirm'd
In the unshrinking station where he fought,
But like a man he died.

SIWARD

Then he is dead?

ROSS

Ay, and brought off the field: your cause of
sorrow
Must not be measured by his worth, for then
It hath no end.

SIWARD

Had he his hurts before?

ROSS

Ay, on the front.

SIWARD

Why then, God's soldier be he!
Had I as many sons as I have hairs,
I would not wish them to a fairer death:
And so, his knell is knoll'd.

MALCOLM

He's worth more sorrow,
And that I'll spend for him.

SIWARD

He's worth no more

They say he parted well, and paid his score:
And so, God be with him! Here comes newer
comfort.

Re-enter Macduff, with Macbeth's head

MACDUFF

Hail, king! for so thou art: behold, where stands
The usurper's cursed head: the time is free:
I see thee compass'd with thy kingdom's pearl,
That speak my salutation in their minds;
Whose voices I desire aloud with mine:
Hail, King of Scotland!

ALL

Hail, King of Scotland!

Flourish

MALCOLM

We shall not spend a large expense of time
Before we reckon with your several loves,
And make us even with you. My thanes and
kinsmen,
Henceforth be earls, the first that ever Scotland
In such an honour named. What's more to do,
Which would be planted newly with the time,
As calling home our exiled friends abroad
That fled the snares of watchful tyranny;
Producing forth the cruel ministers
Of this dead butcher and his fiend-like queen,
Who, as 'tis thought, by self and violent hands

Took off her life; this, and what needful else
That calls upon us, by the grace of Grace,
We will perform in measure, time and place:
So, thanks to all at once and to each one,
Whom we invite to see us crown'd at Scone.

Flourish. Exeunt